# STUDY IN AUSTRALIA PLANNER

# STUDY IN AUSTRALIA PLANNER

Shahina Khan

Vitasta
*Let Knowledge Spread*

Published by
Renu Kaul Verma for
Vitasta Publishing Pvt Ltd
2/15 Ansari Road, Daryaganj
New Delhi - 110 002
info@vitastapublishing.com

ISBN 978-93-82711-78-0


**Disclaimer**

The SiA (Study in Australia) Planner is meant to help students and their families in their preparation towards studying in Australia. It can also be used by counsellors to help students to collect information and store it in one place in a sequential manner. The SiA Planner is to be used as planner guide only. Student is advised to find out valid figures from approved authorities before using them. Opinions expressed in this book are the author's own. The publisher is in no way responsible for these.

Cover Design: Harvinder Bhatia
Layout: Vitasta Publishing Pvt Ltd
Printed at Vikas Computer and Printers, New Delhi

# Author's Note

The SiA (Study in Australia) Planner is not a substitute for professional advice. It is a sincere effort from the author to inform the students aspiring to study in Australia to the best of her knowledge. For this purpose, the author has collected information from multiple sources. A substantial amount of information for the book is collected from the websites of various universities, the Australian government and other private organizations working in this field. The author is not responsible for the accuracy, reliability, and completeness of the material provided either on the website or in the book. As information changes from time to time, the author is also not responsible for any change in the information provided, and not liable for any loss incurred due to information gap or change.

For

Indian students who aspire to study in Australia

# Foreword

I have been involved with the international students from South East Asia, North Asia, the Sub Continent and South America since 1995. For the 22 years, until the present, I have worked extensively throughout India in various roles representing government TAFEs, universities and private institutions. I had Delhi as my base for four years where I spent my time in counseling students and their families.

I have a detailed understanding of the Indian education system, the study goals of the Indian students and the family aspirations and expectations for their children's overseas studies. It is important for families to be involved in the student's planning—basing decisions not only upon the student's strengths, interests and achievements but also upon a discerning appraisal of future trends and career opportunities.

I have had the pleasure of working with Shahina Khan for 18 years, 4 of those years within the same company. I admire Shahina's integrity and commitment to young people who wish to undertake studies overseas to extend their career opportunities. Shahina's commitment to providing comprehensive advice to prospective students, to encouraging them to explore career opportunities extensively and to appraise their interests and capabilities, is unparalleled.

I believe the SiA Planner will assist students and their families in their quest to make the right study choices in Australia.

**Ms Pauline Drayton**

*Consultant with Explore English and MCIE*

# Foreword

If I compare my role as counselling students in India with my expectation from the students when I am judging their application for admission, I find massive lack of preparation expected from a student. Prior to submitting an application, students will need to allow sufficient time to thoroughly research their options with regard to the universities and intended programs that will best serve their academic and career goals. Starting the process early is the best way forward. Instead of doing independent research most students rely on the third party source of information such as agents, family, and friends. While each institution has trained counselor, nothing can replace the self-study and student engagement for successful admission.

I have been a student myself in Australia and completed my MBA from University of Southern Queensland. Before coming to Australia, I travelled extensively in Andhra Pradesh and counselled more than three hundred students from my base in Hyderabad.

In my current role, I am responsible for supporting international student recruitment, including the provision of specialist support and advice in regard to assessment of student entry applications, assessment of qualifications, Simplified Student Visa Framework (SSVF) requirement, arrivals and student enrolment.

I recommend students to conduct independent research that includes course selection, admission, visa application process, studying and living in Australia, estimate the cost of additional educational expenses such as health insurance and travel. As student you can avoid many mistakes and unwanted results by simply being an active part of the preparation and asking right questions from the relevant authorities.

Planners are great tools. The SiA planner is an exhaustive set of material created to assist students with full international admission processes and I would recommend it as an essential tool for any International student to use. SiA planner would allow the student to be fully informed and professionally guided throughout the International education process.

I have worked closely with Shahina Khan and I know her as someone who is a perfectionist in generating student visa applications and guiding and training team members and students. I appreciate her commitment to empower students by sharing the necessary information with them.

**Mrs Ranikanth Sadanala**
*An MBA graduate and student Relationship Officer at University of Southern Queensland, Australia*

# Preface

A world of opportunities opens up for students when they choose to study abroad. It turns out to be a life changing experience not just for the students but also for their families. Among various study destinations, Australia is one of the leading choices that is available. However, only a few students can grab this opportunity either due to lack of information or access to apt guidance that is limited to the major cities. To fulfill this gap, I wrote this book by collecting relevant data that is supported by my nineteen years of experience in guiding students for their higher studies in Australia.

While a lot of information is available on the internet and through other media channels, yet hundreds of students fail either at the initial stages of getting admission or visa for multiple reasons primarily linked to incomplete information or communication gap. Every year, many applications are rejected by the Australian High Commission as the students lack some basic knowledge about the Australian education system, costs involved or the future benefits expected out of their investment of studying in Australia.

The SiA Planner is the first planner of its kind which has been designed to enable students to plan their study in Australia. It not only informs students about various opportunities available in the country but also helps with the admission and visa process along with said and unsaid expectations.

**Shahina Khan**

# Acknowledgement

I am grateful to the people who have been a part of the SiA Planner journey. I am extremely thankful to students who shared their concerns, needs and pitfalls to help educate the new students who are now aspiring to study in Australia.

I am deeply grateful to the people who encouraged and supported me in the planner's creation including Mr Bruce Osborne, Ms Pauline Drayton and Mr Max Radcliffe. I am thankful to Ms Drayton and Mr Radcliffe for reviewing the planner for content and its appropriateness.

I am obliged to Mr Emmanuel Hooson from Vodafone, Mr Scott Wilson from IELTS Online, Mr Francis D'Souza from Westpac, and Mr Ajay Bohora, Co-Founder and CEO of Credila–An HDFC Ltd. Company for their support in making the planner happen. Their contribution and support is noteworthy for the student community.

I am also appreciative of Dr Shabana Khan who reviewed the planner for its effectiveness and aptness. I am obliged to Mr Ashwin Tyagi, from Immigration Hotspot, Australia to share the settlement options with students who are looking at settling down in Australia after their studies.

I am grateful to Ms Beverly Reilly who has worked for more than 15 years with Indian students while representing the University of Canberra and CIT and Mrs Ranikanth from University of Southern Queensland for sharing their understandings with students and their families.

I would like to thank Ms Veena Batra for her competent editing and Ms Renu Kaul Verma for publishing the SiA Planner. I owe huge gratitude to my family for providing me the incessant support in making the SiA Planner happen.

Thinking about studying in Australia?
If you're ready to move, Australia's first bank is ready to welcome you.
Westpac Welcome
200
200 years proudly supporting Australia
Westpac Banking Corporation ABN 33 007 457 141 AFSL and Australian credit licence 233714.
WBC 005

# Contents

## APPENDIX 2: LIST OF THE UNIVERSITIES IN AUSTRALIA



## APPENDIX 3: FORMATS FOR DOCUMENTATION



## APPENDIX 4: SAMPLE LETTERS

## LIST OF TABLES

# Introduction

Education plays a decisive role in everyone's life as it not only dictates the career graph but also lifestyle and choices one makes in life. A quality education thus is not just a need but also an aspiration of millions of students in India. Study abroad brings the hope to fulfill both and students want to go for the best international education. Australia is one of the leading study destinations for Indian students. However, in the absence of adequate information, most students fail to get admission.

In my nineteen years of experience in training counselors and managers to guide students, I realized that the information for study abroad is not just scattered and overlapping but it is also too vast for the students to understand it once as they meet counselors. The students' pace and priority of assessing the information varies immensely. Although majority of the students are given the information in a sequential manner, it has been observed that most students get stuck on some point or the other. The problem areas for students differ and so is the solution. The Study in Australia (SiA) Planner is written to fulfill this gap by providing all the relevant information at one place.

The SiA Planner covers the entire process of decision making for the students and parents when they choose to opt for study in Australia.

It supports students in their course selection, expedites the process of admission, creates an effective visa file and prepares the students well before they leave the country. It also helps students to be aware of the situations and the facts that greatly affect their academic performance in Australia.

Using the SiA Planner will help students avoid major failures caused by negligence or lack of awareness including visa rejection or interview failure. It is designed to educate students with direct information. It also gives access to collect and evaluate the information received from various sources and work along with a counselor to make the appropriate decisions.

## Who should use the SiA Planner?

Every Indian student who is aspiring to study in Australia should use the SiA Planner. The SiA Planner is of great importance to parents who want to send their children for higher studies in Australia. It is highly valuable to the counselors and the institutions helping Indian students to study in Australia also. It supports the counselor's discussion and provides a base for their conversation with students and their families.

## How to use the SiA Planner?

The SiA Planner is meant to support students in preparing their application, and evaluating and assessing it for its success. It gives the facts, resources and relevant information to make right decisions for their admission, visa and settling in Australia. Students can read, make notes and create their application by using this planner.

There are tables created for making notes and space is provided for the issues that need to be discussed with the counselor or the institution. The SiA Planner shares many official links and emphasizes on reading the updated information from the official websites to engage in effective communication with the relevant authorities. You may find some information has changed since the time the planner was created. However, the evaluation criteria may still remain the same.

For documentation, many aspects have been discussed to make students aware of the expectations of the assessing authority. There are generic formats shared for important documentation, which can be personalized and approved from the assigned counselor.

## Chapter organization

The SiA Planner is designed as a step-by-step guide for students to prepare for their higher studies in Australia. It is divided into five different sections and 41 chapters that address various aspects of the process.

The first section of the SiA Planner brings forward the facts related to the education system of Australia. It introduces resources that every student must be aware of. This section also has a table to assess student profile and find out the areas that need student attention for rectification. The section assists students with course selection. It brings forward the popular courses for Indian students and provides important aspects to consider while selecting the course. It also provides information that needs consideration in selecting city and institution apart from exploring the specializations, scholarships and rankings. This section helps you to reconcile your choices and guides you through the decision-making questions.

The second section makes your admission journey a well thought and well planned process. It addresses important aspects of the admission including preparation of documents, application process, and addressing important concerns of admission office. This section shares multiple facts that can help you to expedite the process of admission.

The third section deals with the visa application. It addresses aspects of the visa that each student must be aware of while working on their visa application. The visa section has information related to their GTE criteria, finances, reasons for visa rejection and so on. This section also provides various important formats for the easy reference of the students. There is also a chapter for the married students that addresses criteria of their profile evaluation and documentation.

Section four is meant to help students in their preparation to move to Australia. This section helps students to work on their travel, accommodation, food, clothing and so on. It makes students aware of the various aspects related to living in Australia including communication, health insurance and skills that need to be learned.

The fifth and final section brings forth various important aspects that students need to be aware of before moving to Australia. Knowing about how to deal with cultural differences, changing emotions, finances and time commitment could ease the pressure that students go through. The planner ends with a concluding chapter that summarizes the planner.

# SECTION 1

## Planning for Study in Australia

# 1

# Why Study in Australia?

Australia is one of the important study destinations for the Indian students. In year 2016, 59, 717 Indian students chose to go to Australia for their higher studies. The reason for choosing Australia for your study can vary from seeking sheer quality of education to personal choices, better environment, career growth or future opportunities. Australia offers all of these and much more. This chapter highlights some of these reasons. It is for you to find out your own reason that you need to know before choosing this country for your education.

**Quality Education:** Australia has total 43 universities mostly public and one private and two international universities. According to the 2016 QS World University Rankings, Australia has 7 universities in the Top 100. Besides, twenty-nine Australian universities feature in the top 700. The Tertiary Education Quality and Standards Agency (TEQSA) monitors quality, and regulates university and non-university higher education providers.

**Excellence and Leadership:** Australia has produced 15 Nobel prize laureates in various fields including penicillin, IVF, Wi-Fi, black box and cervical cancer vaccine.

**Easy Facilitation:** According to the 2012 U21 Ranking of National Higher Educational Systems, Australia has the world's 8th best university system ahead of Germany, the Netherlands and Japan. Australia offers flexible pathways programs like English language preparation courses called ELICOS and foundation studies to enter the career of student choice.

**Students' Rights & Safety:** Students' rights are protected by law under the Education Services for Overseas students (ESOS) Act. Students also have access to the Tuition Protection Service (TPS) which is a placement and refund service for international students. It gets activated in the event that your institution is unable to teach your course at any point of time during your studies.

**Better Opportunities:** Many students find better career opportunities in Australia, home country or around the world after having an Australian qualification. Australia provides work permits to international students both during & after studies.

**Better Environment:** An important, attractive factor of Australia is weather and climatic conditions which are similar to India. Besides, most universities are located in cities that offer vibrant international culture that welcomes diversity.

**Family and Friends:** Australia also has a large Indian community that has roots in India and abroad. Many students opt for Australia as they have their relatives and want to stay close to them.

**Career after studies in Australia:** Australia offers great opportunities to develop career after completing your education. It also provides post study work permit to degree students to practice their skills locally and gain Australian work experience.

Thus studying in Australia is beneficial in multiple ways. In your application process, you will be asked for the reasons for selecting Australia as your study destination. Please fill your reasons in the following table.

**Table 1:** Your reasons for choosing Australia for higher studies.

| Ranking | Reasons for choosing Australia |
|---|---|
| 1 | |
| 2 | |
| 3 | |
| 4 | |
| 5 | |

Refer Further Information Section/ Reference for website links from page 225–229.
You are recommended to study the appropriate material beforehand for information assessment.

# 2

# Where to Study in Australia?

Where to study in Australia is majorly influenced by two factors—choice of the city and choice of the institution. Choosing one may influence the choice of the other and reasons vary for individual students. This chapter looks into a few common reasons that may apply to you and the information that you must be aware of when taking this decision.

Although selecting a city looks easy, it is something that needs much more attention than a general knowledge of the place. Each city has a lot to offer to international students. Usually, big cities are famous for many things and are well known, whereas small and not so popular cities offer multiple benefits to students that are not widely discussed. The useful websites to know more about study in various parts of Australia are given in the '*Further Information Section*'.

The Australian states have specialized centers to assist international students for higher studies in their state. You are recommended to use these resources to understand the city's aptness for your requirement. In many regional cities, the cost of living is less and they also offer long-term benefits to students should they decide to stay in Australia. For the purposes of General Skilled Migration, you may be eligible to claim points for the 'Regional Australia' part of the points.

Make sure that you have read enough about your city and record below data to ensure the fulfillment of your requirement. There are links provided with the '*Further Information Section*' which deliver detailed information about different aspects of living and studying in that state.

**Table 2:** Factors that influence your decision of selecting a city.

| Influence | Points to be considered | Yes/ No | Need More Information |
|---|---|---|---|
| Family members or distant relatives | I am sure that I need their help on regular basis. | | |
| Friends | I trust their decisions completely & I am sure that I want to stay close to them. | | |
| Distance | My college is less than half an hour of travelling distance with public transport from the place where I wish to stay. | | |
| Institution reputation | It's exactly what I want. | | |
| Course Availability | The course of my choice is offered. | | |
| Cost of living | The cost of living is within my budget. | | |
| Part-time work opportunities | There are enough part time work opportunities available in the region. | | |
| Regional Australia benefits | My campus location is regional & I will be eligible for regional benefits in case I need it. | | |

## Selecting an Institution

There are 43 universities in Australia which includes one private and two foreign universities. There are many ways of judging an institution to choose the right place for your studies. Any o iteria could lead to a good decision. All you need is to an one parameter to find information before taking the decision.

## World University Rankings

Various organizations have ranked world universities for their quality of teaching and research outputs. These lists can support you in your decision-making for choosing the best university for your education.

**Some of the leading university rankings are:**

1. Academic Ranking of World Universities
2. QS World University Rankings
3. Times Higher Education World University Rankings

These rankings change annually. So, you need to look out for the latest ranking for your university.The ranking websites are provided in the '*Further Information Section*' and the ranking summary is available in the appendix section. Once you finish your reading, use the following table to evaluate the university's ranking value for your education.

**Table 3:** Criteria for evaluating university's ranking for your education.

| Criteria | Yes/ No | Need More Information |
|---|---|---|
| Is the ranking relevant to my requirement? | | |
| Does the ranking directly affect my job placement? | | |
| What is the main reason of choosing the ranking? | | |
| Which ranking is best for my profile? | | |
| Can I choose to study without ranking? | | |

## Australian Higher Education System

An understanding of the Australian higher education system can also help you to identify suitable university in the country.

The Australian tertiary education has two categories. These include universities and Vocational and Education Training (VET) which comprises both TAFEs and the Private Providers. The Tertiary Education Quality and Standards Agency (TEQSA) ensures the quality of Australia's higher education sector. TEQSA registers and evaluates the performance of higher education providers against the higher education standards framework. You may use the TEQSA register to determine whether a provider can offer Australian higher education qualifications, and the CRICOS register to ensure international student's enrolment possibility in a particular course and institution. While selecting a private institution, also use CRICOS register to discover the courses that international students can study and get visa for. Graduate and postgraduate courses are offered by universities, TAFEs, and private providers. The vocational tertiary programs are primarily offered by the Technical and Further Education (TAFE) institutions. TAFE institutes are funded by the state government.

Various groups of the Australian universities are formed who have similar vision. These groups are:

1. Group of Eight (Go8)
2. ATN—Australian Technology Network
3. Sandstone Universities

**Table 4:** Your understanding of the Australian education system.

| Note | Yes/ No | Need to discuss with the counselor |
|---|---|---|
| I am aware of the differences among university, TAFE and private institutions. | | |
| I am aware that I can transfer my studies among universities, TAFEs and private institutions. | | |

**Other Criteria:** For the new universities who do not have rankings, you can study them based on information available on their websites and educational consultancies that work with them. Some of the criteria for which you should seek information to choose your university are given in the following table.

**Table 5:** Collect and assess the following information to choose your university.

| Criteria | Comments | Confirmed | Need More Information |
|---|---|---|---|
| Alumni profiles relevancy | | | |
| Specialization (institution strength in my subject) | | | |
| Subject Accreditation | | | |
| Graduate placements data (for placements similar to what I am looking for) | | | |
| Institution overall profile | | | |
| Relevant ranking/s (if important for my requirement) | | | |
| Group of Universities with similar vision | | | |

Refer Further Information Section/ Reference for website links from page 225–229.
You are recommended to study the appropriate material beforehand for information assessment.

# 3

# What to Study in Australia?

The Australian education system is comprehensive and offers a variety of choices for your study depending upon the level of education you want to go for. The Australian Qualification framework (AQF) has 10 levels, which connects school, vocational and university education qualification under one national education system. AQF qualifications provide flexibility and recognition of previous studies within the system.

**Table 6:** AQF level of qualification and duration of the course.

| AQF Level | Qualification | Usual Duration of the course |
|---|---|---|
| 1 | Certificate I | Non Term |
| 2 | Certificate II | Non Term |
| 3 | Certificate III | 6 months |
| 4 | Certificate IV | 1 year |
| 5 | Diploma | 1 to 2 years |
| 6 | Advance Diploma/ Associate Degree | 1.5 to 2 years |
| 7 | Bachelor Degree | 3 to 4 years |

Contd.

| AQF Level | Qualification | Usual Duration of the course |
|---|---|---|
| 8 | Bachelor Honor's degree | 1 year |
| | Graduate Certificate | 6 months to 1 year |
| | Graduate Diploma | 1 year |
| 9 | Master's degree (coursework) | 1 to 2 years |
| | Master's degree (research) | 1 to 2 years |
| | Master's degree (extended) | 3 to 4 years |
| 10 | PhD/ Doctoral degree | 3 to 4 years |

The qualification levels including the certificate, diploma and graduate diplomas are usually the progression pathways to the degree courses. The certificate I & II qualifications are usually not offered to international students looking for higher education.

## Pathway Studies option

The pathways studies are common in Australia and they are offered to international students as part of their degree qualification. As the name suggests, the pathway studies are offered to the students who are not eligible for direct admission into the degree courses at undergraduate or postgraduate level. The pathway studies are also known as foundation studies and are offered by the providers of all categories including universities, TAFEs and private institutions.

**Undergraduate pathway program levels are:**

1. Certificate III &/ Certificate IV
2. Diploma/ Advance Diploma/ Associate Degree

**Postgraduate pathway program levels are:**

1. Graduate Certificate
2. Graduate Diploma

The pathway programs at certificate level are not offered as an independent qualification to international students unless informed otherwise. The pathway studies help students to prepare well for their progression. Usually there is less number of students maintained in the class as compared to the degree classroom. The students have the opportunity to interact better with the tutor and seek support. During the pathway program (which is usually the first year of studies), you study in a different classroom. The pathway studies are dedicated to students aiming to get into the same classroom in their second year of studies with the direct applicant.

It is important for you to check exact entry requirement of the course that you wish to study at the institution of your choice. If you find yourself short of some of the requirements (mainly academic or IELTS), check the pathway studies availability. The pathway studies also have their entry requirements, which is lower than the direct entry requirement. However, you get the same qualification once you finish your complete degree studies after progressing well into the pathway programs.

The pathway studies are offered by the institutions or specialized pathway providers directly associated and most of the time also located at the campus of the university or college.

**Table7:** Check your entry requirement, before applying for admission.

| S. No. | Name of the University / TAFE/ College that I want to apply for admission. | Entry requirement for direct admission | Marks or the IELTS score that I lack for direct admission. |
|---|---|---|---|
| 1. | | | |
| 2. | | | |
| 3. | | | |

**Table 8:** Check the availability of pathway studies.

| S. No. | Name of the University / TAFE/ College that I want to apply for admission. | Pathway program available for studies |
|---|---|---|
| 1. | | |
| 2. | | |
| 3. | | |

## Course Selection

Australia offers over 22,000 courses across various disciplines, which are accredited under Australian Qualification Framework (AQF). These courses can be classified into those offered at the preparatory foundation level, undergraduate level and postgraduate level. At all these levels there are some traditional and popular choices.

Some of the very popular courses that Indian students choose to study in Australia are:

- Hospitality, Commercial Cookery and Patisserie
- Accounting including Masters of Professional Accounting (MPA)
- Information and Communication Technology (ICT)
- Engineering
- Health courses

Apart from the academic and financial requirements, you should be aware of your personality, interest, and work requirement before choosing a career.

Even though you are expected to have relevant background and good understanding for a course that you want to pursue at the university, it is possible to change your subject specialization or course for a career that you now desire to have. While changing the stream, make sure you know the risk and reason and also benefit of changing the stream. Besides, you need to check for the details of the entry requirement. Entry requirements are given on the university's website where you are planning to study. Make sure you have read and understood the admission requirement and career outcome facts before applying for admission.

There is no perfect way of selecting a course. However, it is critical to learn your requirement very well. Some possible sources for collecting information are:

1. Online surfing, including participating in forums and chat rooms
2. Visiting Australian higher education events and exhibitions
3. Attending seminars organized by various universities
4. Speaking to the counselors and educational consultants

5. Speaking to your friends, extended family members and neighbors about your plans

Once you have chosen your specialization, make sure you have checked the criteria for your confirmed admission. It is expected that you have used most of the resources to collect information about studies in Australia. It is also critical that you are not pressurized or influenced to a level that you should not be by any one resource i.e. your best friend or a close relative. One of the ways to deal with such a situation is to be neutral while collecting the information.

The following table gives some important checklists that you can use to choose your course specialization. You can create such a checklist for your chosen subject too in the space provided.

The following data helps you to be aware of the aspects that need consideration while selecting the specializations.

**Table 9:** Evaluating course information for my career relevance.

| Criteria | Yes/ No | Need more Information from counselor |
|---|---|---|
| The course that I wish to study has good job opportunities in India | | |
| The course that I wish to study gives me skills that are in demand in Australia. | | |
| I have enough background to study the course i.e. I am aware of the entry requirement. | | |
| I am aware of registration requirement to work in Australia or in India after studying my course. | | |

**Table 10:** Your reasons for choosing Hospitality, Commercial Cookery or Patisserie for education.

| Hospitality | Commercial Cookery | Patisserie |
|---|---|---|
| ☐ I love interacting with people.<br>☐ I am willing to work in shifts.<br>☐ I like people from different cultures &nationalities.<br>☐ I like grooming my home & my room.<br>☐ I am prepared for the work demand that may not be glamorous all the time.<br>☐ I like to manage guests and cater to their needs.<br>☐ I can look after unhappy customers in a nice way.<br>☐ ____________ (Your reason)<br>☐ ____________ (Your reason)<br>☐ ____________ (Your reason) | ☐ I like cooking.<br>☐ I can easily stay and cook in a kitchen for up to 2 hours.<br>☐ I enjoy cooking as it is both challenging and creative at the same time.<br>☐ I can deal with meats of all kinds including eggs, fish, beef and pork.<br>☐ I am very attentive as I understand that mishandling of food could be a disaster for my career.<br>☐ I like to know about food products.<br>☐ I enjoy and can cook for very long hours.<br>☐ ____________ (Your reason)<br>☐ ____________ (Your reason)<br>☐ ____________ (Your reason) | ☐ I like sweets more than any other food.<br>☐ I find cooking sweets to be both interesting and creative.<br>☐ I love the demanding responsibility and challenges that comes up with cooking patisserie.<br>☐ I like the challenge of creating new sweets that suit everyone's choice.<br>☐ I am very attentive as I understand that mishandling of food could be a disaster for my career.<br>☐ I like to discover new varieties of sweets.<br>☐ I enjoy and can cook for very long hours.<br>☐ ____________ (Your reason)<br>☐ ____________ (Your reason)<br>☐ ____________ (Your reason) |

**Table 11:** Your reasons for choosing MPA, ICT, Engineering or course of your choice.

| Accounting includingMasters of Professional Accounting (MPA) | Information and Communication Technology | Engineering | (Health or any other subject you choose other than given) |
|---|---|---|---|
| ☐ I have strong accounting skills and knowledge.<br>☐ I am aware that my course has CPA accreditation.<br>☐ I am ready to deal with the heavy accounting data and related financial statements.<br>☐ I know that heavy accounting backend work may not be easy or glamorous.<br>☐ ___________ (Your reason)<br>☐ ___________ (Your reason)<br>☐ ___________ (Your reason) | ☐ I am a technical person and I love computing and networking.<br>☐ My course is accredited by the Australian Computer Society (ACS).<br>☐ I enjoy working in a technical environment finding solutions to technical issues.<br>☐ I know that heavy technical backend work may not be easy or glamorous.<br>☐ ___________ (Your reason)<br>☐ ___________ (Your reason)<br>☐ ___________ (Your reason) | ☐ I am clear that I wish to specialize in the area of my choice.<br>☐ I have studied the regulatory requirements of my career choice.<br>☐ I am aware of the registration requirement of the professional body to practice my skills.<br>☐ I know that heavy technical backend work may not be easy or glamorous.<br>☐ ___________ (Your reason)<br>☐ ___________ (Your reason)<br>☐ ___________ (Your reason) | ☐ I am clear that I wish to specialize in the area of my choice.<br>☐ I have studied regulatory requirements of my career choice.<br>☐ I am aware of the registration requirement of the professional body to practice my skills.<br>☐ I know that dealing with patients and old age people may not be easy or glamorous.<br>☐ ___________ (Your reason)<br>☐ ___________ (Your reason)<br>☐ ___________ (Your reason) |

**My Course Selection for Specialization**

My Course: ______________________________

My Specialization: ______________________________

Career I am looking for: ______________________________

My Course Career Outcome: ______________________________

**Table 12:** Evaluating information to pursue my admission.

| Information | Yes/ No | Need more Information |
|---|---|---|
| I have checked the course structure. | | |
| I know the difficulty level of the course. | | |
| I have the required level of English proficiency to successfully complete the course. | | |
| I have academic strengths to study the core subject that I am taking up. | | |
| The course is approved by the relevant professional body. | | |
| I am aware of the registration requirement if there is any. | | |
| My course provides me the internship if it is required in my profession. | | |
| I have a genuine interest in the career that I am opting to study. | | |
| I am aware of the study hours required per week in my course. | | |
| I am aware of the campus facilities and I can adjust in the big/ small environment that I have chosen. | | |

Refer Further Information Section/ Reference for website links from page 225–229.
You are recommended to study the appropriate material beforehand for information assessment.

# 4

# When to Start Planning for Admission in Australia?

The Australian institutions have two major intakes per year, which means that admissions happen twice every year in Australia in the month of February & July that are also referred to as 'Semester One' and 'Semester Two' respectively. Some highly specialized courses and some engineering streams may have only one intake in a year. This usually starts with Semester one in the month of February.

Some universities also have trimesters, in which the academic year is divided into three sessions. This is usually for the fast track courses for helping students who wish to complete their studies early. Some courses with more number of candidates recur more often e.g.

i. ELICOS intake–Most ELICOS courses start approximately every alternate month.

ii. Foundation Courses usually have three intakes per year

Each intake has two important dates i.e. Orientation Date and Commencement Date. Some applications are also considered for late entry with an extension letter. You must be aware of these details for planning your application.

**Orientation Date:** This is the date by which international students are expected to arrive at the campus. For some institutions, orientation is mandatory to attend.Some institutions allow students to miss orientation and enroll by the latest commencement date. Orientation is very important for students to settle down well and familiarize themselves with the university, accommodation and living requirements.

**Commencement Date:**This is the date when the course studies begin. Many institutions consider this as the last date by which a student must have enrolled in the class.

**Late Entry–Extension Letter:** This allows a student to join classes late. It is highly discouraged by universities as student find it hard to cope with studies if they join classes late.If you may need late entry permission in an emergency, inform the institution in advance and be prepared that some institutions may not allow it.

**Table 13:** Annual Intake Calendar (Start dates) in Australia.

| Month | ELICOS | Diploma VET | Foundation | Degree UG/ PG | Research |
|---|---|---|---|---|---|
| January | Yes | Trimesters | Trimesters | Trimesters | Yes |
| February | Sometimes | Yes | Yes | Yes | Yes |
| March | Yes | Yes | Yes | Yes | Yes |
| April | Sometimes | Sometimes | Sometimes | Sometimes | Yes |
| May | Yes | Trimesters | Trimesters | Trimesters | Yes |
| June | Sometimes | Trimesters | Trimesters | Trimesters | Yes |
| July | Yes | Yes | Yes | Yes | Yes |
| August | Sometimes | Yes | Yes | Yes | Yes |
| September | Sometimes | Sometimes | Sometimes | Sometimes | Yes |
| October | Yes | Trimesters | Trimesters | Trimesters | Yes |
| November | Sometimes | Trimesters | Trimesters | Trimesters | Yes |
| December | No | No | No | No | Yes |

**Note:** Some start dates for semesters or trimesters may overlap with following or previous month. Check updated course start date individually from institution website.

You need to plan your time to ensure starting your studies without any delay. Make yourself aware of intake, deadline and processing time.

## Intake

**Dates:**

1. Two Major Intakes (semester studies) are February and July (mostly 3rd or 4th week of the month). Usually all courses start at this point of time.
2. Minor Intakes for trimester studies begin in January, May, June, September, October and November. Popular trimester courses are Business, Information Technology and Hospitality Management.

**Deadlines:** Although there are no official deadlines for most of the courses, you can only start your studies on time if you apply in advance and keep enough time for further processing of education loan, fund arrangement and visa processing. Some very popular courses in the high-ranking universities have set deadlines for which you need to visit their respective websites.

**Processing Time:** Processing time varies from three days to three months depending upon course and level of assessment required for admission. There is huge variation in processing time. However, a typical time that must be taken into consideration is three weeks.

Masters of Engineering, Fine Arts, Fashion, Medical or Health related admission applications go for faculty assessment before admission officer can issue an offer letter. These admissions may take up to ten to twelve weeks. Under graduate students usually have faster processing time and it varies from one to two weeks or little longer depending upon volume of applications. Applications for credit assessment also take longer time, about four to six weeks.

Processing time also depends on university processing team size and their availability. So to remain unaffected by any situation, it is recommended to provide one-month processing time for an offer letter. **It is, therefore, highly recommended that you should apply about five to six months in advance for admission.**

**Table 14:** Annual Intake Calendar for Your Admission.

| Criteria | Start Dates | End Date Approximately | Start Dates – Counselor Recommendation |
|---|---|---|---|
| I am looking for Admission in the month of | | | |
| ELICOS–if needed | | | |
| Foundation/ Certificate/ pre-masters course if needed | | | |
| Diploma–if taking pathway | | | |
| Degree–Main course | | | |

**I am aware that:**

- ☐ There is no overlapping of dates in my different courses; my main course start date is after the end date of the previous required Foundation or ELICOS course if there is any.
- ☐ The gap is not more than 120 days between my two courses.

# 5

# Cost of Education in Australia

The cost of education in Australia is very high when we compare it with that of Indian education. It is, therefore, very important to plan for it in advance so that it doesn't overwhelm you during the process of admission. The total cost of education in Australia includes fees, travel and living expenses.

## Fee Structure

### Under Graduate Studies

- Universities: AUD 17,500–28,000 per year (depending upon specialization)
- Colleges: AUD 14,500–18,500 per year (depending upon specialization)

### Post Graduate Studies

- Universities: AUD 18,500–30,000 per year (depending upon specialization)
- Colleges: AUD 16,500–22,000 per year (depending upon specialization)

## Living Expenses:

Annual living expenses as per the Australia High Commission visa guidelines are as follows:

- Student or guardian—AUD 19,830
- Partner or spouse—AUD 6,940
- Child—AUD 2,970
- For school aged child—Additional cost for schooling—AUD 8,000
- Schooling cost for the children of PhD student is NIL in case child is enrolled in a government school where tuition fee are waived off.

**Airfare:** The airfare may vary depending on the time of booking. On an average it can cost about AUD 2,000.

**OSHC:** Overseas Health Insurance Cover (OSHC) is required for the full duration of the course. This is mandatory to have before applying for student visa. The cost for OSHC is:

- Single: AUD 500 per year approx.
- Married Student—couple coverage—around AUD 2,600 approx per year depending upon family size and coverage scope.

Apart from these costs there are several costs incurred during the preparation of application, visa and other related needs. The following table notes some of these costs, which may vary from time to time or with institution that you choose to apply for. Therefore, you should put your own cost in the column next to the given cost. Most of the given costs have been taken towards the higher end for better planning. Some of the cost may be nil for you like application fee. Things that are not valid in your case mark them as **NA** or **Not Applicable** like marital status or child visa fee etc.

**Table 15:** Estimated cost to be incurred before leaving for Australia.

| Activity | Details | Average Cost in INR/AUD | My Cost |
|---|---|---|---|
| Documentation | Documents collection, attestation, transcript creation etc. | INR 5,000.00 | |
| Application Fees for admission | As per the institution you apply for admission | INR 5,000.00 | |
| Medical | Confirmed at the time of medical appointment | INR 5,000.00 | |
| Education loan processing fees | Differs from bank to bank | INR 5,000.00 | |
| Visa Fees | Student Visa fee | AUD 550 | |
| | Spouse fees | AUD 410 | |
| | Child visa fees—per child | AUD 135 | |
| Advance payment towards tuition fees | One semester tuition fees | INR 5,00,000.00 | |
| OSHC | Single | INR 75,000.00 | |
| | Family | INR 2,00,000.00 | |
| Air Fare | One way | INR 50,000.00 | |
| Counseling fees | Check from your Counselor | INR 10,000.00 | |
| Accommodation Booking | Check from institution | INR 20,000.00 | |
| Airport pick up | Check from home stay or hostel or person coming to pick you up | INR 5,000.00 | |
| Miscellaneous | Travelling etc. | INR 50,000.00 | |

As you reach Australia, you need to pay for multiple things. In Australia, the living cost varies greatly depending upon the kind of services students use and the city that they plan to live in. Make sure your costing is close to actual money that you would need on arrival. Do not under or over estimate the cost.

**Table 16:** Estimate monthly living cost in Australia.

| Activity | In AUD per month (Approximate) | My Actual Cost as per my city & institute location |
|---|---|---|
| Travel including bus pass | 100.00 | |
| Rent | 800.00 | |
| Food including grocery & eating out | 400.00 | |
| Phone, internet etc. | 50.00 | |
| Electricity | 50.00 | |
| Entertainment | 100.00 | |
| Tuition fees (per emester) | 10,000.00 | |

## About Tuition Fees Payment Planning:

It is important to plan for the tuition fees payment as you pay it in instalments. While the first semester fee is paid from India, usually the time to enroll into and pay for the second semester comes much faster than a student's expectation. It is very important that you note that fee payment date from the academic calendar and not the normal calendar. This is usually within 4 months of your arrival in Australia. You need to fill in dates for your subsequent tuition fees payment.

**Table 17:** Calendar for Your Tuition Fees Payment.

| Academic Calendar | Tuition Fees Amount | Due date for fees payment |
|---|---|---|
| First Semester | | |
| Second Semester | | |
| Third Semester | | |
| Fourth Semester | | |

Contd.

| Academic Calendar | Tuition Fees Amount | Due date for fees payment |
|---|---|---|
| Fifth Semester | | |
| Sixth Semester | | |
| Seventh Semester | | |
| Eighth Semester | | |

## Scholarships

As studying in Australia is expensive compared to India, students are encouraged to explore scholarships that can help to reduce the total cost of education. Australia offers scholarships up to 500 million AUD per year. Some scholarships cover full tuition fees, travel, living, and health expenses while some other scholarships cover only tuition fees. Some of the popular scholarships in Australia are:

### Merit based scholarship:

**Provider** University/ College

**Amount:** Typically 25% of the tuition fees.

**Requirement:** Minimum 75% or above in important subjects and overall performance of the student in interview.

**Which institutions:** Check on institution website at the time of making application. It changes annually at each institution.

**When to Apply:** At the time of Admission.

### The Australian Government Scholarship:

**Provider:** Government

**Amount:** Typically full tuition fees.

**Requirement:** High achievers or top performers preferably with distinctions, specializing in the areas specified for scholarship.

**Which institutions:** Check government website for provider category which is specified as university or TAFE depending upon level and category of the course.

| | |
|---|---|
| **Popular scholarships:** | Endeavour Awards, Australia Awards Scholarships, Australia Awards Pacific Scholarships and Australia Awards Fellowships. |
| **When to Apply:** | Usually 8—10 months before course start date |

## International Postgraduate Research Scholarships(IPRS):

| | |
|---|---|
| **Provider:** | Government |
| **Amount:** | Typically full tuition fees and living expenses |
| **Requirement:** | High Achievers or top performers preferably with distinctions specializing in the areas specified for scholarship |
| **Which institutions:** | Check government website for provider category |
| **When to Apply:** | Usually 8—10months before course start date |

## Bursaries:

| | |
|---|---|
| **Provider:** | University/ College |
| **Amount:** | Typically fixed reductions in tuition fees from 1000 to 5000 A$ per semester or per year. Sometimes these are early bird payment discounts. |
| **Requirement:** | Same as admission requirement of the institution. |
| **Which institutions:** | This may be offered by any institution at any point of time. |
| **When to Apply:** | No need to apply separately; check your offer letter for details. |

You can find information about scholarships at various places. Some of these can be:

- University or College website
- Government Websites
- Newspapers
- Application forms
- Counselors

If you are applying for merit based scholarship or a bursary, look for application requirement at the time of making admission submission. You may have to fill separate application form if you wish your application to be considered for these scholarships. If you decide to apply for an Australian government scholarship, you need around eight to ten months' time to complete the process. Government scholarships are extremely competitive and there are limited seats. Students need to plan well ahead in time and work effectively to gain these scholarships.

## Education Loan

Apart from scholarship, another way to meet your study goal is to apply for an education loan. You will find detailed information about the education loan in later sections. However, you need to start planning about arranging finances at the very initial stages. Refer below article from from Inias's 1st Dedicated Education Loan Company—HDFC Credila to understand benefits that an education loan provides.

### Education Finance

"We have been noticing that an increasing number of students prefer availing an education loan, instead of using up the family's savings to pay the fee upfront. HDFC Credila encourages the students to apply for the loan and have the loan evaluation done even before admission is confirmed. Once the education loan is approved, students can confidently go and apply for their choice of courses and institute, without downsizing their dreams," informs Mr Ajay Bohora, Co-Founder, MD & CEO, HDFC Credila—India's 1st Education Loan Specialist.

**Education Loan Experts Speak:**

Before deciding which entrance tests to take, students and parents look at and explore various parameters. Rank and location of the institute etc. are critical. However, in addition to that, parents and students have increasingly started comparing fee structures of the institutes before deciding which entrance test is to be taken. If the fees of certain institutes are too high, students usually downsize their dreams, and may not even appear for their entrance tests. Usually, parents consider what family savings they have and then make that decision while deciding on the University. However, that need not be the case anymore.

There are specialised lenders like HDFC Credila–who have a pre-approved Education Loan program, where the file processing can be done well in advance. They can tell the students and parents how much education loan will be available to them even before they start applying or start appearing for their entrance tests. With loan funding clarity, students don't have to downsize their dreams; they can confidently pursue their dreams of the best institute available and not compromise on the quality of the institute. It is therefore advisable that students and parents start thinking about applying well in advance for the education loan, around the same time when they are applying to the Universities.

While deciding on education loan, some of the parameters students should pay attention to include:

**Loan Amount:** The amount of education loan the lender is approving. Will it only cover the tuition fees or the entire cost of education including the living expenses? Is there any margin money required (portion of the amount that the students will have to bear)? Lenders like HDFC Credila fund up to 100% of the cost of attendance.

**Tenure of Loan:** The term/tenure of the loan. What would be the EMI on the loan (which is dependent on both the interest rate and the term of the loan). What is the grace period after the graduation before the EMI starts, (time available to students to find the job before the EMI starts)?

**Income Tax Benefits:** An education loan not only funds your higher studies but also helps save tax. The interest paid on the education loan can be claimed as deduction by the student or the co-borrower, as per Section 80E of the Income Tax Act of India, 1961. Under that clause, the repayment of Interest paid on Education Loan is eligible for deduction and moreover there is no cap on the amount to be deducted.Parents are also eligible to claim deduction of interest paid by them on loan taken for their children's education.

**Education Loan comes with lots of other benefits:**

**Proof of funds to secure admission:** To get admission confirmation, a solvency letter needs to be given to show liquid funds. One needs to show liquid funds to cover one-year fee/ first semester fee, depending on the Universitie's requirement, to be able to convince the University about the fee payment capacity to get the Confirmation of Enrolment (COE).

With cost of overseas education ranging between 20-80 lakhs, it's not an easy task to keep such a high amount of liquid funds. Lenders like HDFC Credila provide loan sanction letter before admission, which can be used as a proof of funds.

**Safeguard against cost inflation/fluctuation in currency:** With the fluctuation in the foreign currency, the cost of education can vary up to 20-30%, as experienced recently. It can be tough to produce liquid funds to pay such additional cost. Education Loan from few lenders has flexibility to increase loan amount post disbursement, on fulfilling the required eligibility criteria.

**Getting Visa:** Education Loan sanction letter from an approved lender like nationalized banks or loan specialist HDFC Credila can act as proof of funds for Visa purpose too.

Also, the loan repayment responsibilities are being seen by numerous parents as an opportunity to inculcate the habit of financial discipline in their children. More informed parents also view education loan as an opportunity to help their children build their own credit history on credit bureaus like CIBIL etc.With great repayment track record on education loans, students can avail other loans in the future at competitive rates. All these benefits and ease of application process is making education loans a popular choice among students and parents to fund higher education.

Refer Further Information Section/ Reference for website links from page 225–229.

You are recommended to study the appropriate material beforehand for information assessment.

# 6

# Profile Evaluation

This chapter enables you to evaluate your profile by yourself. Your profile may fall into different categories, each of which has different implications for your admission. The following section gives you various classifications criteria that you need to study and understand in order to create your own profile. Choose the category that is most relevant to your education, and in case of doubt you can email your admission office. It is advisable that you also consult a counselor for final assessment.

Dominant categories and relevant factors for your profile creation are:

**Course:**

A Future course stream matches with my previous academic record or experience or both.

B My course career outcome matches my future career requirement.

C If starting a new stream of studies without having any previous background, I have complete knowledge about the career and reasons of doing so.

D The course that I have selected has excellent job opportunities in home country and rest of the world.

E I am aware of my salary expectation and companies that would hire me in home country and abroad after completing my studies.

## Age:

A Although there is no age restriction on studies, the student needs to have requirement of higher education in their career.

B If the further studies requirement is not clear, student's intention may be considered non-genuine.

C Selecting appropriate course and institution becomes critical if age is beyond normal and gap in studies is too much, usually if it is more than a year.

## Academic Background:

A Second division is the preferable acceptable requirement for successful admission and a visa.

B Third division or low academics students need to prove their ability to study well in Australia.

C Low academic students may start their studies with the pathway programs at both undergraduate and postgraduate levels.

D Highlight your strengths in studies.

## Gap in Studies:

A Gap is a time in which a student is not studying when he is expected to study. If a student is doing something different instead of studying, this must be explained in the statement of purpose.

B It is highly recommended not to frame a story about the gap or create documents or situations which are not true.

C A gap from 6 months to one year is considered normal depending upon student circumstances.

D This is the most misunderstood area; students must clearly specify the real reason of gap(read more about gap in the later section).

## IELTS or English test score:

A An approved English Test Score is required for admission & a visa.

B Without an English language score, a conditional admission application is possible to make.

C Minimum 5.5 band in IELTS score is recommended for successful admission & a visa.

## Marital Status:

A Career requirements of both the partners are assessed.

B The career of the main earning member is considered to be very important. Although this is not the only criterion and application is evaluated in a holistic way giving due importance to the overall student and family situation.

C It is important to convey why a particular spouse's higher studies are more important than the other spouse who is less or equally qualified.

D Spouse must be a temporary entrant like the student.

## Work Experience:

A Ensure that facts given in the experience letter are extremely clear and there is no confusion regarding the role, designation, salary, reporting and so on.

B Do not try to impress by giving more details in the letter which are not true.

C Make sure documents are genuine and coming from the right authority.

D Make sure the documents are verified with utmost care, because mistakes could lead to a rejection at any level.

## Previous Visa Rejection/s:

A Mention each visa rejection in the same or different country.

B Mention category of visa rejection including visitor or permanent residency visa.

C Rejection reasons include lack of documents or any other GTE criteria.

D Serious objections include fraud information given to embassy or breach of visa conditions or being banned in any other country.

## Institution:

A Select an institution that is listed on CRICOS website.

B Check institution website and course prospects.

C Check the grading of the institution.

## Funds:

A Education abroad is heavily dependent on finances. Tuition fees and living costs are much higher than in India. Strong financial planning is needed to get admission and a visa.

B While a set amount of money is required to qualify for visa, a financial arrangement to cover the tuition, living, health insurance and travel cost is needed to prove that applicant can afford higher studies in Australia.

C Family income and savings in India are very important to ensure the financial support.

D Education loan from approved financial institution is recommended.

**Table 18:** Grade yourself on each parameter.

| Parameters | Category ABCD | Details | My Grade |
|---|---|---|---|
| Academic background | A | First Class | |
| | B | Second Class | |
| | C | Third Class | |
| | D | Incomplete | |
| Gap in Studies | A | 6 months or less | |
| | B | Less than a year | |
| | C | Up to 2 years | |
| | D | More than 2 years | |
| IELTS or English test score | A | Same score as required by the institution | |
| | B | 0.5 band less score than required | |
| | C | 1.0 band less than required | |
| | D | 1.5 band or less than is required | |
| Marital Status | A | Single | |
| | B | Married | |
| Age | A | 18 for UG & 21 for PG & 24 for PhD | |
| | B | 19 for UG & 22 for PG& 26 for PhD | |

Contd.

| Parameters | Category ABCD | Details | My Grade |
| --- | --- | --- | --- |
| Age | C | 20 for UG & 24 for PG& 28 for PhD | |
| | D | Much more than required in each category. | |
| Funds | A | Savings, income and education loan–all of the funds are available with the parents. | |
| | B | Savings, income and education loan–all of the funds are available with the parents and extended family members. | |
| | C | Savings, income and education loan–one of the parameters is missing and the available funds are less than required for the expenses. | |
| | D | More than 2 parameters are missing from Savings, income and education loan and finding it hard to arrange funds for the expenses. | |
| Previous rejections | A | Complete documents were not provided in the visa application. | |
| | B | Late application submission or inappropriate course chosen. | |
| | C | Intentions were not genuine or failed in interview. | |
| | D | Fraud or misleading information was given in the file and student was banned. | |
| Course | A | Perfect academic background for the course requirement. | |
| | B | Some academic and experience background is related to the course. | |
| | C | Changing career for better future prospects by studying new course. | |
| | D | Taking up a course for settlement purpose for which there is no background whatsoever to prove interest or calibre. | |

Contd.

| Parameters | Category ABCD | Details | My Grade |
|---|---|---|---|
| Institution grading | A | 1 | |
| | B | 2 | |
| | C | 3 | |

**Table 19:** Consolidate Scores for Your Profile.

| Criteria | Parameters | Category–My Assessment–write ABCD against each | Category–Counsellor Assessment–write ABCD against each |
|---|---|---|---|
| Student Profile | 1 Academic background | | |
| | 2 Gap in Studies | | |
| | 3 IELTS or English test score | | |
| | 4 Marital Status | | |
| | 5 Age | | |
| | 6 Financials | | |
| | 7 Previous rejections | | |
| | 8 Course | | |
| Institution Profile | 9 Institution grading | | |

**My Score:**

As.......................... Bs.................... Cs:.................. Ds:..................

**Table 20:** Profile assessment based on the scores.

| Score | Profile category | What does it mean | How to Proceed |
|---|---|---|---|
| 6 or more As & 3Bs, 0C, & 0D | Excellent | You have an appropriate profile to study in Australia. | Follow intake calendar and start working on your application. |
| 5As , 4Bs, 0C, & 0D | Good | Good chances of getting the admission and a visa. | Follow intake calendar and start working on your application. |

Contd.

| Score | Profile category | What does it mean | How to Proceed |
|---|---|---|---|
| 4As, 5Bs, 0C & 0D | Good | Good chances of getting the admission and a visa | Follow intake calendar and start working on your application. |
| 4As, 4Bs, 1C & 0D | Average | Be cautious & work carefully on your application. | Study intake calendar and start the groundwork for the extra effort required. |
| 3As, 3Bs, 3C & 0D | Average | Be cautious & work carefully on your application. | Study intake calendar and start the groundwork for the extra effort required. |
| 2As, 2Bs, 5C & 0D | Average | Be cautious & work carefully on your application. | Study intake calendar and start the groundwork for the extra effort required. |
| 0As, 6Bs, 3C & 0D | Difficult | Be Extra cautious towards working on your application. | You need to put more effort and time in the preparation. |
| 0As, 5Bs, 4C & 0D | Difficult | Be Extra cautious towards working on your application. | You need to put more effort and time in the preparation. |
| 0As, 0Bs, 9C & 0D | Very Difficult | Make sure you are not wasting time by proceeding further. | Speak to your counselor and take the opinion before proceeding further. |
| 5As, 3Bs, 0C & 1D | Very Difficult | Make sure you are not wasting time by proceeding further. | Speak to your counselor and take the opinion before proceeding further. |
| 3As, 2Bs, 2C & 2D | Very Difficult | Make sure you are not wasting time by proceeding further. | Speak to your counselor and take the opinion before proceeding further. |
| 1As, 3Bs, 2C & 3D | Not Possible | Look for some other option. | Look for some other option. |

Refer Further Information Section/ Reference for website links from page 225–229.
You are recommended to study the appropriate material beforehand for information assessment.

# 7

# Decision to Study in Australia

In the world of information and widely available Internet, it is very easy to gather lots of information, which may make students and their families confused. While it is important to discuss your plans with relevant people, it is important to analyze these opinions critically to avoid taking a decision under wrong influences.

Most people who are successful after studying in Australia may advise students to take up the same subject or a new subject, which has recently become popular. It is critical for students to judge their own academic and financial calibre for ensuring suitability for the course.

You must segregate facts from opinions and personal experiences. Current situation of admission, visa and career opportunities may be completely different from those of your friend or relative who went to study in Australia a couple of years back.

The following table will give you insights into different opinions of your sources of information. It is always better if you are not pressurized for your selection of the course, university or place.

**Table 21:** Evaluating the suggestions for your study in Australia.

| Details | | Suggestion given (Excellent, Good or Not Good) | | | | |
|---|---|---|---|---|---|---|
| **About** | **Details** | **Friends** | **Relatives** | **Online Information** | **Agent** | **University or College** |
| University Course Level | | | | | | |
| Course specialization | | | | | | |
| Career after studies | | | | | | |
| Part Time work during studies | | | | | | |
| Cost | | | | | | |
| Place/ City | | | | | | |

## Decision Making Questions

You need to be sure of some details before finalizing your decision of studying in Australia.

**Table 22:** Criteria for selecting Australia for your education.

| Details | Yes/ No | Need more Information |
|---|---|---|
| I have collected enough information to take the final decision of studying in Australia. | | |
| My tuition fees and living expenses are within my budget. | | |
| My Parents are equally aware of my course and the institution that I have chosen for my higher studies in Australia. | | |
| My decision of studying in Australia is not emotional or influenced by anyone–rather it is a well thought and well planned activity. | | |
| I am aware of work permit conditions after studies. | | |

| Details | Yes/ No | Need more Information |
|---|---|---|
| I am aware of part time work conditions in Australia. | | |
| I am aware of current visa conditions related to my studies. | | |
| My course provides same career outcome as what I am looking for. | | |
| I have a fair idea about the salary that I will be paid in India after completing the course. | | |

## Choice Reconciliation

Record your final choices and compare before applying for admission.

**Table 23:** Choice reconciliation for your admission 1.

| University/ Colleges Name | Tuition Fees (Amount as mentioned on university website) | City Main/ Regional | Accreditation of the course (Yes/ No/Does Not Matter) | Do I qualify for Admission? (Yes/ No/ Need to Check) |
|---|---|---|---|---|
| | | | | |
| | | | | |
| | | | | |
| | | | | |

**Table 24:** Choice reconciliation for your admission 2.

| My Strengths to study course | My weaknesses that I need to improve before proceeding further | Concerns to clarify from counselor / College |
|---|---|---|
| | | |
| | | |
| | | |
| | | |

## Selecting an Agent

Agents play a very important role in helping students to study in Australia. Majority of the agencies representing Australian universities, government TAFEs and quality private institutions are trained by the institutions and are provided with the latest information on regular basis. You may find that the agencies have a lot of information that is useful for not just course selection but also for the faster processing of the admission and a visa.

In India, there is an agent association called AAERI that works closely with the Austrade and Australian and High Commission. The Association of Australian Education Representatives in India (AAERI) assures the integrity and credibility of agents. The AAERI is an independent organization under the Societies Registration Act of India, which was formed in 1996.

The AAERI members across the country, agree to abide by a Code of Ethical Practices (COEP). AAERI's Code of Ethics is based on the Australian Governments' Education Services for Overseas Students Act (ESOS Act). ESOS makes Australian education institutions accountable for the activities of their overseas agents. The AAERI members are required to provide accurate and realistic counselling to prospective students who select Australia as their study destination.You can explore the nearest AAERI agent office by visiting the AAERI website. The following quote will help you to understand the agents role for your admission and visa processing.

The Australian High Commission, New Delhi, India says:

"All prospective students interested in utilizing the services of an education agent are encouraged to utilize the services of an AAERI member."

You may check the agent information on the institutions website where you are seeking admission. You may find a counselor or agent who is independent and who is not a part of the AAERI. In this case you have to be responsible for your decision and the required skill of the person whose services you are taking.

You can get faster admission by making a complete and clear application. Here an AAERI agent is of help as they are trained by the institution and embassy. You can get faster application response, only if your application is clear and complete to the requirement. Irrespective of the method of processing and counselling, your tuition fee remains the same.

The agent receives commission for the services provided to students for admission and visa. This does not impact the student's tuition fees. You will have to pay the same fee if you apply directly to any institution. Sometimes, you may benefit by applying through an agent, as an agent may be able to guide you with the application fee waiver, which is sometimes offered to students applying through the official agencies.

No agent within or outside AAERI can guarantee a visa to the student. The visa decision is not influenced by your agent profile. A good agent is experienced and has knowledge to represent your case to the embassy in an impeccable manner to avoid unwanted results. An official agent has access to the updated information from the visa office and is confident to discuss your case with the embassy if any confusion arises. You must qualify on your own merit to get the visa.

The visa applications are processed on first come first serve basis. Sometimes closer to the intake, the course start dates are also taken into consideration, still the submission date is considered important for the assessment. The complete and clear applications are processed faster than incomplete applications where an interview or further information is required. If your application is incomplete or you need an interview, it will take longer time for processing.

---

Refer Further Information Section/ Reference for website links from page 225–229.
You are recommended to study the appropriate material beforehand for information assessment.

# SECTION 2

## Your Application for Admission

# 8

# Admission Process

Taking admission is a process, which is easier to go through if you are aware of its various phases and components. The following table gives you step-by-step information about admission that you need to know before starting your application.

**Table 25:** Overview of the application process.

| Stage | Action | Details |
|---|---|---|
| Before making application | Collect details | Check entry requirement of the course |
| | | Confirm campus |
| | | Check intake/ course start date |
| | | Application fee–if there is any |
| | | Application type online/ paper application |
| | | Application processing time |
| | | Find out admission interview process |
| | | |

| Stage | Action | Details |
|---|---|---|
| | | Prepare for Interview |
| Application form submission | Fill application form | Complete and cross check your application. |
| After making an application | Wait for acknowledgement | Be prepared for interview. |
| | Be prepared to receive interview call | Keep a track of the processing time of the offer letter. |
| | Wait for offer letter | Start looking at arranging financial requirement of the institution. |
| | Conditional offer letter received | Send required information for unconditional offer letter.<br>Do not pay tuition fee until conditions are met. |
| | Un-conditional offer letter received | Follow instructions for next step–you may need to send financial details or pay the tuition fees for first semester or first year. |
| | Send financial Information | Send the financial information as requested in the offer letter. |
| | Sign acceptance letter | Only available with unconditional offer letter.<br>By signing and sending the acceptance letter to the institution, student confirms the interest to enroll into the seat offered by the institution. |
| | Pay tuition fees | As suggested in the offer letter.<br>Once fees is paid, a COE (Confirmation of Enrollment) is issued which implies that the student admission is Confirmed at the institution. |
| | Pay for health Insurance | Take it for the full duration of the course. It is mandatory to have Overseas Health Insurance for the complete duration of the course before applying for visa. |
| After admission | Proceed to Visa | Prepare visa application. |

Starting an application process requires a good deal of research and documentation knowledge. You need to collect a lot of information to choose the right course, university and city. Once you have chosen these as discussed in previous section (1), the next step is to prepare your documentation. While you may have some documents already, there are many that you need to prepare. These documents are discussed in the following chapters that enables you to prepare your complete admission application.

# 9

# Academic Profile

Academic profile is the first document that you need to prepare while getting ready to apply for admission. This document will have details that you will need to use frequently for filling your admission, visa and many other forms. Make sure you fill in with Accurate and Complete information to avoid rejection.

**Table 26:** Your Academic Profile.

| Degree | Criteria | Detail | |
|---|---|---|---|
| Year X | Overall Grade/ Percentage | | |
| | Division | | |
| | School Name | | |
| | School Address | | |
| | Board/ University | | |
| | Year of Beginning | | |
| | Year of Passing | | |
| | Subject wise Marks | **Subjects** | **Score/ Grade** |
| | 1 | English | |

Contd.

| Degree | Criteria | Detail | |
|---|---|---|---|
| | 2 | | |
| | 3 | | |
| | 4 | | |
| | 5 | | |
| | 6 | | |
| | Overall Score/Grade | | |
| Year XII | Overall Grade/ Percentage | | |
| | Division | | |
| | School Name | | |
| | School Address | | |
| | Board/ University | | |
| | Year of Beginning | | |
| | Year of Passing | | |
| | Subject wise Marks | **Subjects** | **Score/ Grade** |
| | 1 | English | |
| | 2 | | |
| | 3 | | |
| | 4 | | |
| | 5 | | |
| | 6 | | |
| | Overall Score/ Grade | | |
| Bachelor Degree | Full name of the Qualification | | |
| | Specialization | | |
| | Overall Grade/ Percentage | | |
| | Division | | |
| | College Name | | |

Contd.

| Degree | Criteria | Detail | |
|---|---|---|---|
| | College Address | | |
| | University | | |
| | Year of Beginning | | |
| | Year of Passing | | |
| | My Top 6 scores/ Grades through the degree studies | **Subject** | **Score/ Grade** |
| | 1 | | |
| | 2 | | |
| | 3 | | |
| | 4 | | |
| | 5 | | |
| | 6 | | |
| | My failures/ re-appears/ Backlog through the degree studies | **Subjects** | **Score/ Grade** |
| | 1 | | |
| | 2 | | |
| | 3 | | |
| | 4 | | |
| | 5 | | |
| | 6 | | |
| Diploma/ Advance Diploma/ Master's Degree | Full Name of the Qualification | | |
| | Specialization | | |
| | Overall Grade/ Percentage | | |

Contd.

| Degree | Criteria | Detail | |
|---|---|---|---|
| | Division | | |
| | College Name | | |
| | College Address | | |
| | University | | |
| | Year of Beginning | | |
| | Year of Passing | | |
| | My Top 5 scores subject wise through the studies | | |
| | 1 | **Subject** | **Score/ Grade** |
| | 2 | | |
| | 3 | | |
| | 4 | | |
| | 5 | | |
| | 6 | | |
| | My failures/ re-appears/ Backlog subject wise through the studies | | |
| | 1 | **Subject** | **Score/ Grade** |
| | 2 | | |
| | 3 | | |
| | 4 | | |
| | 5 | | |
| | 6 | | |

## Gap in Studies

Your complete timeline from class X is expected to be a normal progression as per country education system. If your progression is not standard and you have a time where you were neither studying nor working, then it is considered a gap in your studies. Four to six months' gap in education is considered normal. If you took a gap of longer duration than this, you are

required to explain the reason.
There are a variety of reasons for gaps. Ensure that you recognize your personal gap and convey it clearly. These reasons may include but are not limited to:

- Busy playing sports or any other extracurricular activity
- Preparing for entrance exams
- Pursuing a hobby
- Wasted time in company of friends
- Working in family business
- Working in friend's business
- Married and looking after family
- Started own business
- Was not doing anything at all, took a break
- Was helping father in agriculture/ business
- Sickness–self or family–most commonly used reason so please provide accurate information
- Crisis–financial or personal–most commonly used so please provide accurate information

These reasons for the gap can be classified into three broad categories:
**1. Study Gaps:** Study gaps include gap between the basic qualification i.e. X, XII, Bachelor's, Master's degree, gap within qualification for reappears and repeat exams etc., and preparation gap (nearly six months considered normal) for entrance test or IELTS test.

**2. Incidental Gaps:** This is not so common as it happens in certain extraordinary situations. However, most students put themselves in this category if they find their previous activity is not relevant to what they want to do in Australia. Some students find it easy to say that they were not doing anything, which is dangerous as it affects student profile assessment. The reality is there is hardly any gap like this except when students underestimate the work they have been doing and try to manipulate it with something that looks good and normal.

**3. Work-related Gaps:** If applicant has been working for more than three to five years and then decides to study in Australia, it brings a question about applicant's requirement of further education at this stage and if applicant is ready to involve himself fully into education after having long gap in education. This is called gap in education and not just gap. Working professionals have a lot at stake when they decide to take a break in their career for higher education. The career break will have other impacts on their profile. It is critical to justify how the career break will add value to their career after the time and money spent on education.

There are huge assumptions around filling gaps in studies and it is one of the most mishandled situations in student applications. In order to make the application look good, many students decide to manipulate their situations. Once you do that, you come into the same category of other hundreds of students giving the same reason and you get rejected on one of the most generic reasons used by the college or embassy.

The series of questions that you may be asked may include the following:

**1. What were you doing during the period when you were not studying or working?**

The question may seem frightening. However, the answer is very simple. A student must know that while this gap reveals that the student has spent time without doing anything, the institutions are looking for genuine answers. Fake or manipulated answers are easy to catch and can become one of the reasons for the rejection of your admission or visa.

**2. Why do you want to study in Australia now?**

This question comes as a surprise as it is a completely new and future focused question. Your future planning and preparedness has the main importance in your admission and visa process. So you don't have to link your gap with the future aims.

**3. How to answer about the gap?**

You should always tell the truth about your study gap. Telling the real reason which is your personal one and cannot be copied attracts more positive response from the institution.

Common perceptions about gap: There are some common perceptions about the gaps that you must be aware of:

- I cannot go to study in Australia if I have gap in my studies.
- I must provide a good reason even if it is not the real reason.
- I need to create fake experience letter to fill the gap.
- I may generate fake medical certificates to prove that I was sick or my father was sick.

The gap reality is that a gap is a situation that requires clarification with some evidences. This helps the institution and embassy to know the student better. It is the future prospects and student capability to study the course academically and financially that decides the success of student admission and visa.

**Documents that you may be asked to present for your gap in studies to the institution:**

- Admit card/ examination entrance card for the test preparation taken.
- IELTS/TOEFL/GMAT/ GRE preparation card or exam card or previous score card.
- Medical treatment papers in case of severe medical issues.
- Marriage certificate.
- Participation certificate or news cuttings if pursued some sports or hobby at school, state or national levels.
- Any other official proof available.

# 10

# English Profile

When a student starts planning to study in Australia where English is the first language of communication, it is expected that the student has enough English skills to complete the course successfully. There are various ways to show your English skills ability. A few common methods used by the institutions to judge the language ability include:

1. Academic scores in English subject in class X and XII.
2. If student has studied throughout in English medium both in school and college.
3. An official English skill test.

While the first two methods provide an indication that student may have good language ability for the admission and visa purposes, the Australian institutions and embassy primarily relies on the official English skill test scores for judging student's English ability. The popular tests used for this purpose are:

1. International English Language Testing System (IELTS): This is the most common test used for both admission and a visa in Australia.
2. Occupational English Test (OET).
3. Test of English as a Foreign Language Internet-Based Test (TOEFL iBT).

4. Pearson Test of English (PTE) Academic.
5. Cambridge English Advanced (CAE) test (also known as Certificate in Advanced English).

You may like to take any of the above mentioned tests. Each of these tests judge four language skills:

1. Speaking
2. Listening
3. Reading
4. Writing

To score high on these aspects, the students are required to prepare and practice these skills. Many students score less due to inadequate preparation. There are many ways to prepare for the English test. Depending upon the training requirement, you may take up personal, online or classroom trainings. There are many online training packages available for students that include both study and practice information.

The level of the preparation required for your English test depends on your existing skills that you can assess by using the following table.

**Table 27:** Your existing English skill.

| Criteria | Details | Validity criteria for English Test Exemption | Have I got enough scores for the test exemption? |
|---|---|---|---|
| Marks scored in English in Class X | ________ | ________ | ________ |
| Marks scored in English in Class XII | ________ | ________ | ________ |
| I have studied in English medium throughout my studies | ________ | ________ | ________ |

## English profile based on test score:

My overall test score: ______________________________

Name of the test: ______________________________

Date of appearing for the test: ______________________________

**Table 28:** Your English skill test scores.

| English skill | My scores | University/College Requirement | Score that needs improvement |
|---|---|---|---|
| Speaking | | | |
| Listening | | | |
| Reading | | | |
| Writing | | | |
| Overall | | | |

## In case of poor English skill

Most courses require students to have competent or proficient level in the English test. If your English skill is lower than the level you require, you may be eligible to study an English course in Australia before starting the main course. Such courses are called ELICOS or EAP.

1. English Language Intensive Course for Overseas Students (ELICOS): ELICOS provides English language training for the students who wish to build their English skills before starting their main course.
2. English for Academic Purposes (EAP): The EAP course is similar to the ELICOS and it develops academic language skills for the natives of the non-English speaking countries like India.

Please note that both ELICOS and EAP have separate tuition fees and it also increases the duration of the course. ELICOS/ EAP is not a part of the main course. Studying ELICOS/ EAP increases your cost of tuition and living expenses. It is cheaper to study English in India and improve the test score.

### Exemptions for English test

An official test score is highly recommended for the faster processing of the admission and a visa. In certain cases, an English requirement exemption is granted by the institutions for some brilliant students who have performed extremely well in their studies. You should not apply for exemption unless you are sure that you qualify much beyond a minimum requirement. You must be fully aware of the English exemption requirement of the institution before making a request for exemption. If your request is denied, you may waste a lot of your time.

The students who can apply for the English test exemption in Australia are:

1. Students who are enrolled in a full-time school studies as a principal course as:

a. Secondary Exchange Programs
b. Postgraduate research courses
c. Standalone English Language Intensive Course for Overseas Students (ELICOS)
d. Foreign Affairs or Defense sponsored students

2. Students who have completed at least five years study in one or more of the following countries

a. Australia
b. Canada
c. New Zealand
d. South Africa or
e. The Republic of Ireland

3. Citizens and passport holders of one of the following English-speaking countries

a. Australia
b. Canada
c. New Zealand
d. South Africa or
e. The Republic of Ireland

4. Students who have successfully completed their studies in Australia in the English language, so they have either

a. The Senior Secondary Certificate of Education, or

b. Studies at the certificate IV or higher level within two years prior to making an application for the student visa.

You must practice as much of the testing material as possible. Many students score less than their actual capability due to lack of preparation. You may find free practice material online. However, you are recommended to enrol and use the structured and professional material for preparation. You can get information on the official websites of the recommended tests and the specialized preparation centers.

---

Refer Further Information Section/ Reference for website links from page 225–229.
You are recommended to study the appropriate material beforehand for information assessment.

# 11

# Statement of Purpose

Statement of Purpose (SOP) is a very important document in your application. It conveys that the applicant has an appropriate profile for the chosen course and institution. A strong SOP reflects that the student is Genuine and Temporary Entrant (GTE) and his intention is to successfully complete his/her studies in Australia. It also conveys that the student has the ability to complete his/her studies and will abide by the visa rules and regulations without any interruption. While some universities do not ask for SOP, if you have to write one, then it is an opportunity to present your case strongly in front of the admission and visa officers.

A good SOP should convey the following messages:

- ✓ Student is GTE (Genuine & Temporary Entrant).
- ✓ Student knows career outcomes in India and abroad after studies.
- ✓ If student is married, spouse is also GTE (Genuine & Temporary).
- ✓ Student is not faking or manipulating any information in the SOP.
- ✓ Student has written it himself.
- ✓ Student deserves admission on the basis of information provided.

## Do's of SOP:

- ✓ It is short and concise.
- ✓ It has highly personalized information.
- ✓ It has only relevant information.

## Don'ts of SOP:

- ✗ It is either too long or too short.
- ✗ Using abbreviations for common words.
- ✗ Repeating sentences.
- ✗ Giving reason like "this course will give me excellent career" without explaining what career.
- ✗ Writing non-relevant things as the course outcome.
- ✗ Giving irrelevant quotes at the beginning.
- ✗ Course outcome is different from what is given on university website.
- ✗ Writing course name incorrect or writing only half course name.
- ✗ SOP is written by someone else.
- ✗ Poor English and grammar mistakes.
- ✗ Mismatch between IELTS score and SOP language.
- ✗ Not signing the SOP.

**Preparation for writing SOP:** Before starting to write SOP, you need to find out complete information about your university, course, admission, visa and your future career. The following checklist will help you to retrieve all relevant information.

**Table 29:** Details you need to know before writing SOP.

| Details | Status |
|---|---|
| I have visited website of my university or college. | |
| I understand course structure, course content, fees structure and most importantly, career outcomes. | |
| I have read testimonials on the website. | |
| I know location and exact campus where I am seeking admission. | |

Contd.

| Details | Status |
|---|---|
| I also know other universities offering same course in the same city. | |
| I have specific reasons why I have chosen this university over the others. | |
| I am looking for the same career outcomes that the course provides. | |
| I can afford the cost of my education in Australia. | |

Once you have gone through the details, then start answering the following questions, which will help you to write your personalized SOP.

**Table 30:** Details of your personalized SOP.

| My criteria | Details |
|---|---|
| My reasons for choosing to undertake the course of study specified in my application. | |
| My reasons for choosing my education provider. | |
| My reasons for choosing to study in Australia rather than home country. | |
| The relevance of my course of studies to my academic and/or employment background. | |
| The relevance of my course to my future career/educational plans. | |
| The kind of employment I will be seeking on my return to home country. | |

For your reference, sample SOPs are given in the Appendix.
Your Statement of Purpose

Once your SOP is complete, check against following points:

- ☐ My profile is clearly stated in the SOP.
- ☐ My intention for the higher education requirement is conveyed successfully.
- ☐ I have clearly conveyed that I am GTE (Genuine & Temporary Entrant).
- ☐ I have complete knowledge about the course and I am aware of my course requirements.
- ☐ My course is appropriate for my aspired future career.
- ☐ The course career outcome is same as what is given on the institution's website.
- ☐ SOP size is reasonable.
- ☐ The SOP is clear, concise, and complete in sentence structure.
- ☐ I have written the SOP.
- ☐ I have signed and dated the document.

# 12

# Letter of Recommendation

The letter of recommendation (LOR) is an important document that helps the admission team to understand applicant's strength and suitability for the program. A letter of recommendation, as its name suggests, is a one-page recommendation written by someone who is holding a responsible position in an organization and knows the applicant's academic background enough to suggest that the choice of course is valid and useful for the applicant's career and growth. The person who writes a recommendation is called a referee. A referee should know the applicant well enough to give recommendation. If the referee doesn't know the applicant for long or too well then he/she should mention that in the letter.

It is important to remember that LOR is a very personal document and it must remain personal to your profile. A LOR makes your skills visible to the selection committee for admission. These skills can be either academic or professional. Therefore, there are two types of recommendation:

a. Academic, and

b. Professional

One may need to give one or both depending on the course and academic profile of the applicant. Generally, 2-3 letters of recommendation are needed for the admission purpose. So, it is very important to read instructions on what kind of recommendation is required and how many.

A letter of recommendation is submitted along with application form for admission. Applications for most master's degree courses require an LOR. Some courses ask students to directly send LORs, in which case students have the liberty to attach LORs given by the teacher or professors. On the other hand, most online application forms ask for referee contact details whereby a confidential reference questionnaire is sent to the referee to respond to. A referee may be contacted very soon through email or phone depending upon admission process of the institution. A referee needs to answer the questions responsibly in case the university sends a questionnaire form to be filled. A more detailed reference is considered to be a good recommendation.

There are multiple characteristics of a good recommendation. These may include but are not limited to the following:

- ✓ A referee should mention duration and nature of his/her association with the applicant.
- ✓ A referee should have his/her faith in the applicant's capabilities.
- ✓ The skills mentioned in the letter should be relevant to the course and show applicant's suitability.
- ✓ A reference letter should have 2-3 paragraphs i.e. it should not be too brief or too long.
- ✓ The language should be formal and precise.
- ✓ The letter should have complete address and contact details of the referee.
- ✓ It may be given on a letterhead.
- ✓ The letter should clearly specify the designation of the referee.
- ✓ Any additional information about referee that will help build credibility.

**Things to cover in the letter of recommendation for academic background:**

- ☐ Academic skills and achievements, such as hard work, dedication, leadership and so on.

- ☐ Class participation/ enthusiasm.
- ☐ A memorable incident or project completed within class.
- ☐ Uniqueness of student's personality.
- ☐ The qualities of the student that qualify him/her to be a good candidate for the course.
- ☐ The positive aspects and work of the student during his/her contact with the referee.
- ☐ Some characteristics or defining qualities of the student.

Things to cover in the letter of recommendation for work experience:

- ☐ Professional characteristics, such as responsibility, enthusiasm, problem solving skills, team work.
- ☐ Awards & recognition
- ☐ Roles & responsibilities
- ☐ Reputation with colleagues and seniors
- ☐ Duration of association
- ☐ Capabilities & skills
- ☐ Knowledge & creativity
- ☐ Intelligence
- ☐ Performance under pressure.
- ☐ The qualities of the applicant that qualify him/her to be a good candidate for the course.
- ☐ Any other positive aspect and work of the applicant during his/her contact with the referee.

## LOR Data for Application Form

Many universities ask for specific details about your referee. Please fill the following details in your application form. The tables ask you to fill more information which will also help your referee to write about you.

**Table 31:** Your academics data 1

| Criteria | Details |
|---|---|
| School/ College Name | |
| Qualification/ Subject studied | |
| HOD or Professor or Teacher who knows me well | |
| My performance at the school | |
| My Achievements | |
| My friends know me as | |
| My authorities consider me as | |
| My Extra-Curricular Activities | |
| Referee details I need<br>☐ Full Name<br>☐ Designation<br>☐ Address<br>☐ Email<br>☐ Mobile | |
| I have informed my referee on DATE: | |
| Referee updated contact details: | |

**Table 32:** Your academics data 2

| Criteria | Details |
|---|---|
| School/ College Name | |
| Qualification/ Subject studied | |
| HOD or Professor or Teacher who knows me well | |
| My performance at the school | |
| My Achievements | |
| My friends know me as | |
| My authorities consider me as | |
| My Extra-Curricular Activities | |

Contd.

| Criteria | Details |
|---|---|
| Referee details I need<br>☐ Full Name<br>☐ Designation<br>☐ Address<br>☐ Email<br>☐ Mobile | |
| I have informed my referee on DATE: | |
| Referee updated contact details: | |

**Table 33:** Your experience data 1

| Criteria | Details |
|---|---|
| Company Name | |
| Duration | |
| Designation | |
| In-charge or Senior who knows me well | |
| My role and responsibility | |
| My Achievements at work | |
| My colleagues know me as | |
| My seniors consider me as | |
| Referee details I need<br>☐ Full Name<br>☐ Designation<br>☐ Address<br>☐ Email<br>☐ Mobile | |
| I have informed my referee on DATE: | |
| Referee updated contact details: | |

**Table 34:** Your experience data 2

| Criteria | Details |
|---|---|
| Company Name | |
| Duration | |
| Designation | |
| In-charge or Senior who knows me well | |
| My role and responsibility | |
| My Achievements at work | |
| My colleagues know me as | |
| My seniors consider me as | |
| Referee details I need<br>☐ Full Name<br>☐ Designation<br>☐ Address<br>☐ Email<br>☐ Mobile | |
| I have informed my referee on DATE: | |
| Referee updated contact details: | |

**Table 35:** Your experience data 3

| Criteria | Details |
|---|---|
| Company Name | |
| Duration | |
| Designation | |
| In-charge or Senior who knows me well | |
| My role and responsibility | |
| My Achievements at work | |
| My colleagues know me as | |
| My seniors consider me as | |

Contd.

| Criteria | Details |
|---|---|
| Referee details I need<br>☐ Full Name<br>☐ Designation<br>☐ Address<br>☐ Email<br>☐ Mobile | |
| I have informed my referee on DATE: | |
| Referee updated contact details: | |

# 13

# Experience Letter

Experience letters basically give details of your profession or work related roles and responsibilities that you may have undertaken before seeking admission to the course. It is important to follow the guidelines for its acceptance by both the university and visa office. While most institutions have their own format for an experience letter, you can create your own letter and request your organization to provide you with complete information. Since the experience letter is a professional document, it needs to be written carefully. You will be using this document for a long time in future so it is worth putting time and energy into it.

In general, an experience letter is the most misused document and for this reason it invites a lot of scrutiny by both the admission and visa processing officers. Many students create false experience letters to fill their study gaps, which is easy to find out by the authorities. Some organizations also create fake experience letters and charge for it. Since this has become a common practice, each letter is carefully scrutinized for being a fraud. Some of the ways for checking validity of an experience letter may include:

- Direct/ Indirect verification (checking from 3rd party if they know the person).

- It may be checked more than once.
- Verifying data from other teams or reception or neighbors.
- Telephonic or personal verification.
- Unannounced visit to office in case of distrust.
- Use client photo to find out if neighbor/ other officers or lift boy recognize the applicant.

It is critical that you make sure that each and every aspect of your experience letter tells the truth. It is much easier to handle a situation arising out of not working than a lie. Consequences of fake experience letters are severe. Some of these may be:

- Rejected for admission.
- Ban to apply for future admission in the university.
- Visa rejection.
- Ban to enter into Australia.

**Content of the letter:** It is important that you have the required contents covered in your experience letter. Some of the critical information that an experience letter must cover is:

- ☐ Applicant's full name
- ☐ Working hours (full time/ part time)
- ☐ Duration
- ☐ Designation
- ☐ Responsibilities
- ☐ Promotions/ Achievements/ Other activities
- ☐ Technologies used (in case of technical work)
- ☐ Salary (as appropriate)

Some other critical elements of the experience letter are:

- ☐ It should be written on the company's letterhead.
- ☐ It should have updated contact details with landline numbers.
- ☐ It should have correct and complete employer name (if company's trading name is different).
- ☐ The data should be complete and crisp.

- ☐ It should be a one-page document.
- ☐ It should use correct English and grammar.
- ☐ It addresses the document appropriately.
- ☐ It is signed by appropriate department with right authority.
- ☐ It has company stamp.
- ☐ It is dated appropriately.

# 14

# Filling Form & Submitting Application

While filling application form is a simple data processing activity, some students find it a very scary process. Awareness makes it easy; make sure you know about forms before starting to fill one.

| Topics | Note |
|---|---|
| Latest Valid Version | Use latest valid Application Forms. Check date before downloading. |
| Correct Application Form | Use Only International Student Form. |
| Check Application Fee | Not all institutions take fees. Check if fee waive off is possible. |
| Filling Application form | Follow instructions. |
| Do not leave Anything Blank. | Write Yes/ No/ NA–Blank means you have missed or not read information. |
| Student Name | As per passport. |
| DOB | As per passport. |
| Personal Details–Address | Current address where you are staying NOT passport address if it's different. |
| Personal Details–Email ID | It should be a valid students email ID. |

Contd.

| Topics | Note |
|---|---|
| Agent Details | Your representative's address or stamp. |
| Country of citizenship & country of birth | As per passport copy. |
| Program Details | ❖ Program Name<br>❖ Course code<br>❖ Course Duration<br>❖ Intake/ Start Date<br>Details must be taken correctly from University website–Application will be put on hold if details do not match with university data. |
| Intake & Campus | As per course information on the institution website. |
| Credit Transfer | If yes, please provide syllabus. |
| Education Summary | As per mark sheets. |
| English Proficiency | Chose options appropriately. |
| Employment History | As per the experience letter. |
| Checklist | Check each box appropriately at the end. |

## Documents Checklist

Student Name: ______________________________

University: ______________________________

Course: ______________________________

Intake: ______________________________

Update/ Creation Date: ______________________________

**Table 36:** Document checklist.

| Tick-availability | Document | Comments |
|---|---|---|
| ☐ | 10th Mark sheet | |
| ☐ | 10th Passing Certificate | |
| ☐ | 12th Mark sheet | |
| ☐ | 12th Passing Certificate | |

Contd.

| Tick-availability | Document | Comments |
|---|---|---|
| ☐ | Degree–Semester 1 | Consolidated mark sheets are not accepted. |
| ☐ | Degree–Semester 2 | |
| ☐ | Degree–Semester 3 | |
| ☐ | Degree–Semester 4 | |
| ☐ | Degree–Semester 5 | |
| ☐ | Degree–Semester 6 | |
| ☐ | Degree–Semester 7 | |
| ☐ | Degree–Semester 8 | |
| ☐ | Backlog Mark sheet | |
| ☐ | Backlog Mark sheet | |
| ☐ | Backlog Mark sheet | |
| ☐ | Backlog Mark sheet | |
| ☐ | Backlog Mark sheet | |
| ☐ | Backlog Mark sheet | |
| ☐ | Provisional Degree Certificate | It must be issued from the UNIVERSITY not from College. |
| ☐ | Degree | From University only. |
| ☐ | Diploma–Semester1 | Consolidated mark sheets are not accepted. |
| ☐ | Diploma–Semester2 | |
| ☐ | Diploma–Semester3 | |
| ☐ | Diploma–Semester4 | |
| ☐ | Diploma–Certificate | From the Affiliation Body only–check embassy requirement. |
| ☐ | Passport Copy | Check information for spelling mistakes and data discrepancy of any kind. |
| ☐ | Recommendation Letter 1 | Find out number of recommendations required from the institution. |
| ☐ | Recommendation Letter 2 | |
| ☐ | Recommendation Letter 3 | |

Contd.

| Tick-availability | Document | Comments |
|---|---|---|
| ☐ | Application Fees | If Needed. |
| ☐ | Gap in Studies | Make sure that the gap is ADDRESSED & no false information is created to fill this gap. |
| ☐ | Marital Status | Registered Marriage Certificate. |
| ☐ | IELTS/ TOEFL/ PTE score | Updated Score–not more than 2 years old. |
| ☐ | English Medium Letter | Education and examination both conducted in English. |
| ☐ | Application Form | Correct and UPDATED form is used. |
| ☐ | Application Form | All the forms are filled completely. |
| ☐ | Documents Attested | All the above documents are attested by the authorized representative or Notarized. |

Once you have all the documents at one place, you can submit your application either directly through online application system or through your counselor. Once it is submitted you must wait for your admission interview or your offer letter. The details of the admission interview are discussed in the following chapter. To get the offer letter in time, you need to make sure that you have done the following:

✓ Apply in advance to avoid last minute rush.

✓ Send complete documents at once.

✓ Follow application instructions carefully.

✓ Avoid sending any extra information which is not relevant.

✓ Respond to queries quickly with complete information at once.

**For Further Information:**
Check the admission link of your institution carefully.

# 15
# Admission Interview

It is likely that once you submit your application for admission, the admission officer calls you for the interview. They do that after assessing your academics and English capability. While the interview seems to be a scary matter for a student, it is rather an opportunity for students to convey their interest in getting the admission. The interview is basically conducted with the intention to get complete details and clarity about the student. It is the admission officer's responsibility to ensure that the genuine applicant has been given admission in the class. Along with academics, it is critical for the admission office to find out if you have chosen the right course and have done all required preparation to study in Australia. If you lack any preparation including English ability, course selection clarity or your finances to complete your qualification, there will be high chances of your admission denial. Speaking to the student provides clarity to the admission officer that student is capable and genuine to come and study in Australia.

Admission interview can happen any time after the submission of your admission application. It is usually done next day or within a week's time depending upon the volume and availability of the admission team and institution's processing time. Most of the interviews these days are conducted through Skype calls where the institute personnel can see the applicant and observe body language along with student's knowledge and preparation. Some institutions may also call students directly on their mobile number to interview.

Students are expected to have done a thorough research on the course of their interest and should be clear about their future prospects after completing the course. In the interview, they may be asked for the following:

- ☐ Career objectives
- ☐ ROI (Return On Investment) of studying in Australia.
- ☐ ROI of studying a similar course in India.
- ☐ English ability to study the chosen course.
- ☐ Intention for going to Australia is studies and not to work or get settled there.
- ☐ Student has enough resources to fund his education without being dependent on part time work income.
- ☐ Student MUST be GTE (Genuine and Temporary Entrant)
- Genuine means the focus is studies only with clear career pathway.
- Temporary means the student has good career prospects in India after studies. Student plans to come back after studies although he has an option to work or settle down in Australia if wishes to do so.

## Interview Preparation

To prepare for the interview, you need to read about your course, university and Australia as much as possible from varied resources. Make sure that you are prepared before taking the interview. If you are not prepared you may give random answers, which implies that you are not serious about your studies and you have not put effort in the preparation. There are many resources available on internet to prepare for the interview and it is suggested that you use at least three to four different sources to understand different aspects of the same question. The following table gives you some interview related questions. You should search and try to answer them for yourself. Do not give memorized answers, and explore all kinds of details to get clarity. Make sure you have understood the purpose for each question. Answer only after listening to the complete question.

**Table 37:** Your interview questions.

| Questions | Your answers |
|---|---|
| Why are you interested to study in Australia? | |
| Why do you wish to study this particular course? | |
| What are the career opportunities in India after completing studies in Australia? | |
| What kind of remuneration do you expect to earn in India after your studies? | |
| Name a few companies where you would be applying for a job? | |
| What designations would you apply for after studies? | |
| No one hires a fresh graduate for a senior position. Why do you think that you can become a______by just getting this qualification? | |
| Which other institutions in Australia offer a similar course that you are thinking of applying for or have already applied to? | |
| Why have you chosen________ specialization when you have scored a 3rd division in the same subject in India? | |
| Do you think that you can cope with studies in Australia? | |

Contd.

| Questions | Your answers |
|---|---|
| What are the study commitments of your course? | |
| Can you name the subjects that you are going to study? | |
| What kind of the research have you done before finalizing your course and institution? | |
| Who motivated you to choose this course and college? | |
| Who is sponsoring your studies? | |
| What is your parents' profession and what is their annual income? | |
| What are the personal liabilities of your sponsors? | |
| Why is a distant relative giving you money when his own income is just enough to support their family? | |
| What is the family structure of your sponsor and what are his liabilities? | |
| What is the relationship with your sponsor? | |
| Do you have authentic proof of your relationship with your sponsor? | |

Refer Further Information Section/ Reference for website links from page 225–229.
You are recommended to study the appropriate material beforehand for information assessment.

# SECTION 3

## Your Visa Application

# 16

# Overview of Visa Application

As you would know, visa is the critical requirement for your entry into Australia. Unlike many other countries, the Australian student visa is not stamped in the passport anymore. You will receive your visa in email and you will need to take a printout to travel and carry passport along. This also means that you do not need to submit your passport to the embassy for a visa stamp.

To get a successful visa, it is important that you know the particulars of your visa application and follow the guidelines accurately. A successful visa application is the one that covers each aspect of the visa requirements such that the visa officer is not left with any questions to ask. It is the role of the embassy to ensure that applicant has genuine intention to study in Australia. You may think that you have the right intention but if your application doesn't convey that, you may have to answer the same questions in the interview. Although majority of the documents and questions are repeated for visa, there are new perspectives added at the time of visa application that you should be aware of.

The Australian student visa framework is known as Simplified Student Visa Framework (SSVF). The SSVF has classified the Australian institutions (Universities/ TAFEs / Private Colleges) known as the education providers in three categories where one is streamlined but for the other two categories students are required to provide higher evidentiary requirement for a visa. You can find the risk rating of your university or college at the DIBP website.

The SSVF also has three categories for country assessment separated by country risk ratings where immigration risk one is streamlined and two and three require higher evidences. Depending upon the risk rating of the country and the education provider, the documentary evidence requirement is decided. India has the immigration risk rating of three. This means that the Indian students need to provide evidence of their English language and financial capacity to study at any of the level two and three education providers. Read the table below to understand the evidence requirement.

**Table 38:** Country risk rating and evidentiary requirement.

| Requirement Level | Education Provider Immigration risk | Country Immigration risk rating of INDIA | Possible evidentiary requirements | Comments |
|---|---|---|---|---|
| Lower Evidentiary requirements | One | Three | Generally these students would not be required to provide evidence of their English language or financial capacity. | You may still be asked to provide evidence of English and finances both so please keep them ready. |
| Higher Evidentiary requirement | Two | Three | Generally, these students would be required to provide evidence of their English language and financial capacity. | Provide all the requested documents to university and the embassy. |
| | Three | Three | | |
| Genuine Temporary Entrant requirement—continues to apply to all the applicants | | | | |

The SSVF also has 2 subclasses for student visa:

- Student Visa Subclass 500: All the students apply for student visa in this category regardless of their level of course.
- Student Guardian Visa Subclass 590: This is for students who are under 18 years of age. In this case student's guardian/parents apply for the visa if they wish to accompany the child.

## Filling Visa Form

The process of making the visa application is online. Although you may choose your agent or consultant to fill your form, it is recommended that you are fully aware of the visa forms requirements. The students are expected to collect the information and keep the documents handy before starting to fill up the visa application online. Your medical tests should be done before applying for the visa.

In your online visa application, you will be required to answer the questions related to your reasons to study in Australia. You must prepare this answer well in advance. The answers to these questions help the visa officer to understand your preparedness and personal motives to choose Australia as your study destination. The questions may have space limit. While filling the form, you must:

- ✓ Answer each question correctly and completely.
- ✓ Do not leave anything blank.
- ✓ Read instructions and questions accurately before responding.

## Documentation

Accurate documentation is important to have a successful visa for Australia. To make your visa application, you need to submit the following documents:

1. Passport details (scanned notarized copy of the full passport).
2. Confirmation of Enrollments (COEs) (You must confirm your seat for each course enrolled in till the highest qualification).
3. Academic transcripts (class X onwards, mark sheets and passing certificates).
4. Proof of your English language ability (IELTS score sheet).
5. Medical report.

6. Overseas Student Health Cover (OSHC).
7. Financial documents (Fully approved education loan letter, sponsorship or any other financial support for your study).
8. Documents to prove that you will stay in Australia temporarily.

After you have gathered and scanned the documents that support your application, create an account and apply for your student visa with online application system on

https://www.border.gov.au/Trav/Visa/Appl/Student

Along with your application, you are also required to pay the visa processing fees. There is a separate visa fee for all the members included in the visa application. You should arrange a credit card for online payment of the visa application fees. Once you submitted your application, you may be called for an interview. The overall processing time varies from four to six weeks which may go up to twelve weeks. You will receive your visa through email.

---

Refer Further Information Section/ Reference for website links from page 225–229.

You are recommended to study the appropriate material beforehand for information assessment.

# 17
# Passport Check

You may have seen your passport many times by now. However, it is critical to have a final check of all the details before applying for a visa. You need to ensure that you have a VALID PASSPORT. Tick each box to ensure that your passport is intact.

**Table 39:** Passport check.

| Passport check | Tick box if applicable |
|---|---|
| Passport has validity for more than a year and it is not expiring soon. | ☐ |
| Your name, including parents and spouse is spelt correctly. | ☐ |
| Passport is not torn or scratched or wet. | ☐ |
| All passport pages are intact and there is no missing page. | ☐ |
| All the particulars in the passport are correct including date and place of birth. | ☐ |
| If passport is changed after applying for visa, you must ensure linking your new passport to the visa application. | ☐ |

You are not required to submit original passports for yourself or family. You need to submit the NOTARISED copy of the FULL passport. If you are married and travelling with children, you need to submit notarized copy of complete passport of each person included in the visa application.

**NOTES**

# 18

# English Skills for Visa

Since Australia is an English-speaking country, sufficient English language skills to complete the course successfully is one of the basic requirements of a visa. The visa officer is concerned about anything that may possibly disrupt the student's education in Australia and your English language ability is an important part of the visa processing. You may believe that you have enough English skills to communicate well; nonetheless it is the level of the course and complexity of the subject that is taken into consideration for assessing your English skills.

Your English skills are assessed on the following criteria:

1. Your scores in the English Eligibility test.
2. Marks scored in the English subject in class 10th and 12th.
3. Response to the questions asked in the visa forms.
4. GTE statement.

The students who score less in the IELTS opt for the ELICOS before starting their main course. Please note that studying ELICOS increases the course duration and also the tuition fees. The ELICOS tuition fees is charged in addition to the main course fee.

If you are going to study a course that requires external registration for practicing, you must check the requirements and find out how much effort you need to make for reaching the required score. You may have to take up longer duration of ELICOS for reaching that level. Please note that the course will require a very high level of commitment, time and money. You should focus on achieving the essential level of the English score from India itself as it is cost effective to improve English skills in India.

The English eligibility test is the best tool for the assessing officer to judge your English language ability. The other factors including the English scores in class X and XII and answers in the visa form and GTE statement etc., reinforce the fact that student has the capability to study the course successfully in Australia.

# 19
# Medical Checkup

One of the important requirements of the Australian student visa is the medical checkup. Students are required to go for medical examination with immigration panel physicians of the Australian High Commission. The students are required to take an appointment with the listed doctors to undergo necessary medical checkup.

Once your appointment with the physician is confirmed, you need to carry the requested documents with you. This includes but is not limited to:

1. HAP ID (applicant unique ID created while filing online form)
2. Original Passport
3. 3 Photos
4. Any previous medical records
5. Offer Letter
6. Medical Fees
7. Spectacles

**Table 40:** Your preparation for medical checkup.

| Requirements | Details |
|---|---|
| Appointment Date | |
| Appointment Time | |
| Hospital/ clinic Address for medical | |
| Dr FULL NAME | |
| My HAP ID | |
| Documents that I am carrying | ☐ Original Passport<br>☐ 3 Photos<br>☐ Any previous medical records<br>☐ Offer Letter<br>☐ Medical Fees<br>☐ Spectacles |

You are recommended to get your medical checkup done about a week before submitting your visa application. An online system known as eMedical processes health examination results electronically and forwards it to DIBP for assessment. Refer to the websites given in the "*Further Information Section*" for panel doctors and HAP ID creation.

---

Refer Further Information Section/ Reference for website links from page 225–229.
You are recommended to study the appropriate material beforehand for information assessment.

# 20

# Overseas Student Health Cover

The Overseas Student Health Cover (OSHC) is an insurance for the international students, essential to meet their medical and hospital care costs. The OSHC is a compulsory requirement for studying in Australia. All overseas students travelling on student visa to Australia are required to have OSHC for the full duration of the course. The student dependents including spouse and children are also required to have OSHC for the complete duration of the course. The students are required to buy OSHC at the time of paying the tuition fee and before applying for a visa.

The medical costs in Australia are very high, and a single health issue may place a student in great financial trouble and could affect studies and budget. An OSHC provides protection by covering the costs incurred during your visits to the doctor, some hospital treatments, ambulance cover and medicine costs. Students also have an option to take higher range policy, which is comprehensive and has more coverage for extra services.

## Cost of OSHC

The cost of OSHC depends on the type of the coverage taken. The average cost of the cover is AUD 500 for 12 months' singles cover, AUD 1,400 for 12 months' couples cover, AUD 2,000 for 12 months single-parents cover and AUD 2,300 for family cover. The coverage amount changes frequently and it must be checked from the provider at the time of finalizing the insurance policy. A student must read the coverage provided by their insurance provider carefully to understand what is paid for. There are many avenues to buy OSHC including study abroad consultant, university or college and online portals.

## Process of using the insurance

A General Practitioner known as GP is the first person you will visit if you are unwell in Australia, except in the case of an emergency. In case of emergency, dial 000. A GP may provide you with a prescription for medication or refer you to a specialist. While making an appointment with the GP, mention the insurance policy that you hold and carry your OSHC card. You can choose to visit any GP or specialist in Australia. However, if you choose your OSHC partnered places, you will benefit with cashless facility. The normal policy is that a GP refers you to the specialist.

## Billing process

When you visit a doctor or a specialist you will most likely need to pay upfront, either before or right after you get the treatment unless you have visited a partnered or OSHC preferred place. OSHC Preferred Providers are the medical centers, general practitioners, radiologists and pathologists who have agreements with insurance companies. Using these providers means that they will bill insurance provider directly for student visit to GP.

Depending on the plan you have chosen, you may still have to pay a gap or co-payment on the day of your visit to the Provider. This may occur if the charge is more than the benefit you are entitled to under your cover. In these instances, you will not be able to claim extra money paid from the insurance company.

Source: https://www.nib.com.au/overseas-students

## OSHC providers

Some of the leading OSHC providers are:

- Australian Health Management
- BUPA Australia
- nib OSHC
- Medibank Private
- Allianz Global Assistance

You can select a new provider and transfer your insurance if you are not satisfied with the existing OSHC provider. You may incur a 'refund processing fee' if you transfer midway through a period of cover. If you have paid in advance, you can get a refund. Only Australian registered private health insurers can offer OSHC. This is because the Australian Government wants to be able to monitor and regulate insurers covering people living temporarily in Australia.

To activate your OSHC card you need to call on the number provided in your information pack and give your accommodation information within couple of days of your arrival. You will receive your OSHC card on the Australian address provided.

**Table 41:** Summarize your OSHC options.

| Details | My Notes | Counselor Recommendation |
|---|---|---|
| OSHC Provider Name (suitable to my requirement) | | |
| Plan I need (Coverage provided) | | |
| Cost of the complete plan that I have chosen | | |
| Date of Buying OSHC cover | | |
| Place of Buying OSHC | | |
| Questions I need to ask from counselor/ provider | | |
| Contact number of OSHC provider/ Customer service | | |

Refer Further Information Section/ Reference for website links from page 225–229.

You are recommended to study the appropriate material beforehand for information assessment.

# 21

# Financial Requirements

You are required to submit the particulars of your financial arrangements in your visa application. The visa officer assesses your financial status against the visa guidelines. The intention of the sponsor for the funds availability to the student during studies is assessed through the visa application. The visa officer's objective is to find out if the student has the accessibility of the essential finances at the time of the payment of the tuition fees and the living expenses.

In case of category 2 and 3 education providers, student will need to demonstrate financial capacity in any one of the following ways:

1. Evidence of funds to cover travel to Australia and 12 months' living, course and (for school aged dependents) schooling costs for the student and accompanying family members.
2. Evidence of meeting the annual income requirement.
3. An Acceptance Advice of Secondary Exchange Students (AASES) form for secondary exchange students only.

It is the availability of the finances throughout the education duration that is taken into consideration; however, you would need to show financial documents only for first year of expenses. This is because people cannot have liquid money or deposit fee in the account for the full duration of the course. It is beneficial to show that the student and his/her sponsor have arranged finances to cover the expenses until student completes the education. Along with documents, it is the intention of the students and their sponsors, together with financial planning that plays a major role in the decision-making.

You could estimate your financial accountability for the visa application by using the following criteria.The compulsory 12 month living costs for the visa applicants are:

- Student/guardian–AUD 19,830
- Partner/spouse–AUD 6,940
- Child–AUD 2,970

**For situation1:** Evidence of funds to cover travel to Australia and 12 months' living, course and schooling costs (for school aged dependents) for the student and accompanying family members is required.

For a single student, the funds requirement will look like:

| | |
|---|---|
| Tuition Fees for 1 year (as per offer letter): | 22,000.00 AUD |
| Living expenses for student for 1 year (as mentioned by DIBP): | 19,830.00 AUD |
| Travel cost (as mentioned by DIBP): | 2,000.00 AUD |
| OSHC (As mentioned in the offer letter): | 1,500.00 AUD |
| Total: | 44,880.00AUD or 22, 44,000 INR |

(At the rate of 1AUD=50INR)

Thus a student needs to show INR 22,44,000.00 as readily available money to the embassy.

**For situation 2:** Evidence of meeting the annual income requirement.

In this scenario, the student is required to provide annual income of at least AUD 60,000 per year of his prime sponsors who are parents or spouse.

For students accompanied by family members, the amount must be AUD 70,000 or more per year.

The income must be the personal income of the student's spouse or parents only. In situations where both the student's parents are working, their combined income can be considered. In all cases, the evidence of annual income must be provided in the form of official government documentation including Income Tax Returns.

- School aged children expenses will be required to show 8,000 AUD if they are included in the student visa application.
- The children of the PhD students are not required to demonstrate evidence of the schooling costs if they provide evidence of enrolment in an Australian government school with exemption of school fees.

## Sponsors

The sponsors are very important for managing your higher studies expenses in Australia. It is vital for you to understand who all can sponsor your expenses for your studies. Your sponsor could be:

- Self
- Spouse
- Parents
- Bank
- Grandparents
- Siblings and their spouses
- Distant Relatives – Maternal or Paternal Uncle/ Aunt/ Spouse family
- Friends
- Neighbors
- Any other person

Most of the time, it is a combination of two to four categories of the sponsors who come together to sponsor the student's education abroad. It is one of the embassy's roles to ensure that the students and their accompanying family members have genuine access to the required funds provided by the student or their sponsor or both.

Many student visas are denied despite providing enough sponsors and lots of sponsorship documents. Major attention is given to the fact that money shown in the student visa application does not seem to be **actually available to the student** during their studies. This means that students may show money in the application but their sponsor also has lot of personal liabilities and their income and savings are just enough to look after their family. Also, the chances are high that money shown by the sponsor may not be given to the student when he/she will need it.

The following issues are taken into account while considering the funds availability:

- The **nature of the relationship** between the student and the person who is providing the funds.
- Income, assets and employment of the student or the other person who is providing the funds.
- Previous visa history of both the student and the person providing the funds.

While anyone can be a genuine sponsor, there are some specifications that would help you choose your sponsor.

- ☐ Parents/Self/ Spouse **(highly recommended)**
- ☐ Education Loan **(highly recommended)**
- ☐ Grandparents–Maternal/Paternal (**Considered** depending upon sponsor income and situation).
- ☐ Siblings/sibling spouse (**Considered** depending upon sponsor income and situation).
- ☐ Uncle / Aunt–Maternal/Paternal (**May be considered** depending upon sponsor income and situation).
- ☐ Friends/ Family Friends/ Neighbor etc. (**Hard to be considered** depending upon sponsor income and situation).

Each Sponsor needs to provide following details on their affidavit of support.

- Why are they sponsoring the student?
- When and how they want the student to return their money, if they want it to be returned?
- How much of the amount declared will be used to sponsor the student?
- What are their own financial liabilities?
- Information about their profession and family responsibilities.
- Details of the sponsorship given to any other child in the last two years.

Sponsor identity and financial details are needed as:

- Income proof/ ITRS of the Sponsor (last three years).
- Photo ID proof (passport copy, driving license etc.)
- Relationship proof with the student.
- Bank Statement of the last 5 months.
- Other financial investments to prove financial capability to sponsor student.

## Relationship proofs of Sponsors:

It may appear strange to prove your relationship with the sponsor; however, this is a compulsory document of your visa application. Studying in Australia is expensive and if someone decides to help you financially for your education, the person must be very close to you to give you that kind of money.

Unfortunately, a lot of manipulations happen in the area of sponsorship and many non-genuine sponsors are also found in the visa applications. Hence, all the sponsors and applications are scrutinized carefully for being genuine.

For the fast processing of your visa application, you must provide authentic and clear documents for the evidence of relationship with your sponsor. With each sponsor, evidence of relationship with student is essential. You may use one or more documents to provide relationship with the sponsor:

- Voter ID Card/ Aadhar Card
- Passport Copy
- Birth Certificate
- Year 10th Passing Certificate
- Registered Marriage Certificate
- Driving License

In case of no relationship with your sponsor, you need to provide details in the affidavit of the support. You need to state reasons for which the person is sponsoring you even if he is not a blood relation. Since it is a big financial investment, the sponsor's commitment and financial capability is very important. If the sponsor's intention is not conveyed effectively, your visa may get rejected on the basis of lack of available finances as it may appear that the money shown in the file will actually not be accessible to you at the time of studies.

Judge your sponsor's capability well before asking for their sponsorship. Answer following questions:

- Is my sponsor capable of giving me the money that I need?
- When do I need to return this money, if it is given interest free?
- If it is a gift from the sponsor–is the sponsor rich enough to give a gift of such a big amount?
- Will my sponsor be actually able to give me the money when I need it during studies?

Table 42: Details of your sponsors.

| **Details of your sponsors** | |
|---|---|
| **Sponsor Number 1** | |
| Name | |
| Relationship with student | |
| Is relationship proof available | |
| Documentary evidence of the relationship | |
| Sponsor Occupation | |
| Income per year | |
| Proof available for income–last 3 years | |
| Savings in the bank account | |
| Property/ies | |
| Liabilities–Children or other loans | |
| Why sponsoring? (personal/ emotional reasons) | |

Contd.

| Details of your sponsors | |
|---|---|
| **Sponsor Number 1** | |
| How much funds are ready to give to student | |
| Which activity is sponsored like Tuition/ OSHC or Living etc. | |
| **Sponsor Number 2** | |
| Name | |
| Relationship with student | |
| Is relationship proof available | |
| Documentary evidence of the relationship | |
| Sponsor Occupation | |
| Income per year | |
| Proof available for income–last 3 years | |
| Savings in the bank Account | |
| Property/ ies | |
| Liabilities–Children or other loans | |
| Why sponsoring (personal/ emotional reasons) | |
| How much funds are ready to give to student? | |
| Which activity is sponsored like Tuition/ OSHC or Living etc. | |
| **Sponsor Number 3** | |
| Name | |
| Relationship with student | |
| Is relationship proof available | |
| Documentary evidence of the relationship | |

Contd.

| Details of your sponsors | |
|---|---|
| Sponsor Occupation | |
| Income per year | |
| Proof available for income–last 3 years | |
| Savings in the bank Account | |
| Property/ ies | |
| Liabilities–Children or other loans | |
| Why sponsoring (personal/ emotional reasons) | |
| How much funds are ready to give to student? | |
| Which activity is sponsored like Tuition/ OSHC or Living etc. | |
| **Sponsor Number 4** | |
| Name | |
| Relationship with student | |
| Is relationship proof available | |
| Documentary evidence of the relationship | |
| Sponsor Occupation | |
| Income per year | |
| Proof available for income–last 3 years | |
| Savings in the bank Account | |
| Property/es | |
| Liabilities–Children or other loans | |
| Why sponsoring (personal/ emotional reasons) | |
| How much funds are ready to give to student | |

Contd.

| Details of your sponsors | |
|---|---|
| **Sponsor Number 4** | |
| Which activity is sponsored like Tuition/ OSHC or Living etc. | |

## Income Statement

Income statement is an important document in your visa application. A good income helps the visa officer to recognize the financial capability of the sponsor. It is important that you understand the documents that are required by the embassy to comprehend the income of the family. If ample proofs are not provided with the visa application, it may lead to incorrect evaluation.

Your sponsor may have more than one source of income. It is important to mention each income in the file and compile appropriate documents. Refer following list to understand the documents that you need to request from your sponsor.

Please note that the visa officer needs to see each document in your application to distinguish the complete financial strength of the sponsor.

## For Agricultural Income:

Although the agriculture income is tax exempted, the Income Tax return declaring the agricultural income is the acceptable document. Others are:

- ☐ Land ownership
- ☐ Translation from authorized translator if the documents are not written in English
- ☐ Account statement of where the agriculture income is deposited — print out on bank letterhead

It is very hard to judge the agriculture income on the basis of the traditional documentation available including:

- ☐ Income Certificate from Tehsildar
- ☐ J forms

### For Salary Income in India:

- ☐ Income Tax Returns of the last 3 years—notarized copies

### For Salary Income from abroad:

- ☐ Salary account statement
- ☐ Salary slips for the last 3 months
- ☐ Passport copy and visa details
- ☐ Sponsorship letter from local notary of the country of stay (Refer format for full details)
- ☐ Annual Income Tax file of the last 3 years

### For Business Income:

- ☐ Business registration details & Certificate of Incorporation—notarized copy
- ☐ Balance sheet brief for the last 3 years of company—notarized copy
- ☐ Income Tax Returns of the company—notarized copy
- ☐ Bank statement of the company for the last 4 months—print out on bank letterhead
- ☐ No objection letter from the other partners in case business income is shown—original
- ☐ Personal Income Tax Returns—notarized copy
- ☐ Personal savings statements and relevant documentation—print out on bank letterhead

### For Pension Income:

- ☐ Proof of Retirement Documents—notarized copy
- ☐ Pension account statement showing credit of the pension amount for the last 4 months—print out on bank letterhead.
- ☐ Details of family members and other dependents.
- ☐ Proof of source of any other income (if there is any).

### For Rental Income:

- ☐ Proof of ownership of the property—notarized copy
- ☐ Lease Deed—notarized copy

- ☐ Income Tax Returns for the last 3 years.
- ☐ Account statement where rent is deposited—print out on bank letterhead

## For Dairy Income:

- ☐ Proof of ownership of the dairy
- ☐ Account statement of where dairy income is deposited—print out on bank letterhead
- ☐ Although the dairy income is tax exempted, the Income Tax return documents declaring the dairy income is an acceptable document.

## For Interest Income:

- ☐ Interest income should be a part of the Income Tax Returns—notarized copy
- ☐ Copy of fixed deposit or bank document—notarized copy
- ☐ Bank letter on bank letterhead mentioning the duration and amount of the original deposit and interest earned annually—original.

## Income from part-time work in Australia

The financial requirement of the education and living expenses in Australia is sometimes underestimated by the students and their families. The students occasionally believe that they can earn money by working part-time and sponsor their studies and living expenses. This is a highly overestimated situation. Mostly students are paid the minimum wages for the unskilled work they qualify for and the money they receive is only enough to support their pocket money. If they are skilled enough to find skilled work on the basis of their caliber and experience, they may be able to partially support their living expenses. However, this earning is not counted towards the funds availability requirement of the visa application. The students usually have limited time to work after attending their classes and managing their basic necessities of cooking, cleaning and other household chores. A student visa is for studies and the focus must remain studies.

## Education Loan

Many parents and even the institutions prefer education loan as a great way to secure finances for the student. Study in Australia is expensive and taking an education loan takes extra pressure away from the sponsor. Besides, the education loan interest is lower as compared to the other private loans and it provides a lot of flexibility towards the repayment. It provides the sponsor peace of mind and allows the students to freely focus on their education. It also provides assurance to the visa and admission officer about the financial security of the students to complete their education successfully in Australia. It is, however, not mandatory.

Education loan must be taken from the education loan providers approved by the Australian High Commission. Most banks listed on the Australian embassy website provide education loans. You need to find out if you or your parents are already holding a personal account with any of these banks. Most banks are happy to provide education loans to their existing clients as that helps them to know the customer quickly. Also, the bank should be within easy reach of the parents for future transactions. Apart from the official processing time guideline, a lot depends on the branch team, its loan authority and schedule of the bank. Some banks are quick and they can process education loans within couple of weeks to a month's time while many others take up to three months depending upon their processes and speed.

For education loan, most banks ask for an admission letter, which is the offer letter. You should have an unconditional offer letter before the approval of the education loan. You also need to collect data about your living expenses in Australia. Most relevant details are listed in your admission letter. If not, links are mentioned in the offer letter. Read each link to demonstrate information to your bank. Some banks also ask for university brochures. Make sure you have online details with you as the world is going paperless and you may not find brochures available. You can apply for the education loan as soon as you receive an offer letter from the university.

**There are some critical steps involved in taking the education loan. These steps include:**

1. Query: finding interest rate, exploring academic and financial eligibility requirement of the bank.
2. Preparation: Arranging offer letter, expenses details plus security required for education loan.

3. Evaluation: If property is mortgaged.
4. Applying: Making application for education loan.
5. Verification: Bank verifies information provided.
6. Decision on application: approval/ denial
7. Issuance of education loan: if it is approved.

## Documents required for the education loan approval for the visa application:

1. Education Loan letter.
2. Copy (notarized) of the documents submitted against security/ mortgage.
3. Relationship proof of guarantor with student.
4. Loan disbursement letter for the money already used towards the payment of first semester tuition fee.

Most banks need security for providing the education loan and it is mostly property or fixed deposits. While property is most popularly used for an education loan, it needs proper evaluation from approved evaluator from the bank. Some sponsors decide to make a fixed deposit and take education loan in order to keep money with them.

There is a limited amount of education loan that you may be eligible to get without any security if you qualify with its requirement. Usually student academics and guarantor financial strength and banking history are taken into consideration. Since studying in Australia requires a lot of money, most students go through the security process. Bank priority of giving the education loan works on many parameters. It is recommended you speak with two to three banks before finalizing your options.

Some students also opt for a personal loan for studies but it is important to note that interest rates of personal loans are very high and repayment policies are not flexible as compared to the education loan. Unless there is good income or financial support available towards the repayment, taking personal loan for education is not recommended.

## Education loan letter for visa:

Once you have gone through the complete process of taking the education loan, please provide full information that you wish to be printed on your education loan letter. Each bank has its own format and while each one is complete in its own way, embassy needs data in a straightforward manner. You should share what you want to have on your education loan letter. This will help you with faster processing of your visa application. A general format of the education loan letter may include the following:

**Letter must be issued on the updated bank letterhead with below details:**

- ☐ Complete bank address
- ☐ Current bank phone numbers including land line.
- ☐ Bank email address
- ☐ Stamp
- ☐ Bank Manager's signature and complete name.
- ☐ It is recommended to get the loan issued on bank head office letterhead from someone who has direct authority to issue education loan.
- ☐ In case education loan is issued by the local branch with authority from respective head office, head office contact details are also required for verification purposes.

**Content of the education loan letter should include:**

- ☐ Purpose of the loan: higher education in Australia only
- ☐ Category of the loan: education or personal loan
- ☐ Fully approved Loan: no conditions attached
- ☐ Complete amount of the education loan
- ☐ Margin money required
- ☐ Must be issued in student's name
- ☐ Co-borrower's details
- ☐ Security provided/ Mortgage details
- ☐ Interest rate
- ☐ Repayment plan

## Do's:

- ☐ Start enquiring early about the education loan.
- ☐ Have complete documents ready as prescribed by bank.
- ☐ Keep a copy (preferably notarized) of all documents submitted at bank.
- ☐ Have education loan letter issued with complete information.

## PF/ GPF/ EPF

Some students also use PF/ GPF or EPF deposits to manage their finances for studying in Australia. Once you decide to use these deposits, you must ensure meeting the related terms and conditions. Read following extract to evaluate your decision of using provident fund as source of funds available for your higher studies in Australia.

"Savings accounts maintained with a commercial bank under schemes such as the Public Provident Fund (Amendment) Scheme would satisfy the definition of 'money deposits with a financial institution'. This is because monies in these savings accounts are accumulated from deposits made by the individual (or on their behalf) and are held by an entity that satisfies the definition of 'financial institution'.

There is however the question of genuine access to funds, when dealing with accounts under this scheme. There needs to be clear articulation of the financial institution holding the funds and what is available to the applicant through a loan or withdrawal, not simply what is held. Ideally, any withdrawn money is stored in an account that does not restrict access.

An Employee Provident Fund that can be linked to the applicant could be considered an acceptable source as long as the case officer is satisfied that they(students) have ongoing access."

With these deposits the visa office needs to be satisfied that student has continuous access to the money.

## Post Office Deposits

"A Post Office does not meet the definition of a "Financial Institution" and therefore these are not considered acceptable as evidence of financial capacity."

22

# GTE Facts, Criteria and Evaluation

Satisfying Genuine & Temporary Entrant (GTE) criterion is one of the basic visa requirements. While your statement of purpose or GTE statement provided in the admission application may have provided this information already, the GTE statement has utmost importance at the time of making the visa application.

A typical GTE statement needs to address certain specific questions. All the questions are generic in their stand but they need your specific and personal answers. Find out your personal reasons for selecting the course, institution and country.

1. Make available an authentic answer relevant to your situation and your personal circumstances.
2. Do not ask a third person about what is a good answer; think yourself by following the guidelines.
3. There is no perfect answer to the GTE questions. You may not satisfy the visa officer even if you give the best answer if it is not found relevant to your requirement.

## GTE Questions:

1. **What are your reasons for choosing to undertake the course**

**of study specified in your application?** Selecting a course where you are going to invest lakhs of rupees and years of your life, is the critical part of studying abroad. You must be sure about the reason of choosing the course. If changing the stream, why are you changing the stream? Why do you think that this course has better career prospects than your past studies?

**Your reasons may include:**

- You achieved excellent scores in a related subject e.g. if you are going for an accounting course, you have got distinction or first division in the accounts subject.
- The course you have chosen provides the relevant national and/or international registrations to practice as a professional.
- Demonstrate your passion for the course and career that you have chosen.
- The course structure gives you an edge to practice your career.

**2. What are your reasons for choosing your education provider?** Why have you chosen a particular university or college?

Your reasons may include:

- Location.
- Budget.
- Ranking.
- Department strength.
- Scholarships given to students, or
- Any other reason which is highly personal to your requirement.

**3. What are your reasons for choosing to study in Australia rather than in your home country?** There are many destinations providing similar education and career prospects—why have you chosen Australia? Is it really worth studying in Australia?

**Your reasons may include:**

- Personal reference (family/ friend).
- Weather conditions.
- Proximity to travel.

- Course/ Subject specialization.
- Safety and Security, or
- Any other reason which is highly personal to your requirements.

**4. What is the relevance of your course to your academic and/or employment background?** Do you have enough academic/ work skills to study the course successfully in Australia?

**Your reasons may include:**

- Excellent past academic scores.
- Relevant past work experience.
- Career progression route knowledge and future it promises.
- Thorough knowledge of the course structure, what it requires and what it offers.

**5. What is the relevance of the course to your future career/ educational plans?** Have you calculated Return on Investment (ROI) for time and money both spent in Australia? Do you know what kind of jobs and salaries you would get after completing your studies in Australia?

**Your reasons may include:**

- Excellent career jump in India (expediting career growth).
- Outstanding career opportunities abroad in other developed countries.
- Admirable salary hike; you may mention name of the possible organizations, expected salary structures and targeted designation etc. However, make sure you have studied data before using it. Find out facts before quoting anything.

**Table 43:** My details for GTE criteria to be evaluated.

| Points to be answered | My facts |
|---|---|
| Course I wish to study | |
| Tuition Fees-Total | |
| Tuition Fees-Annual | |
| Tuition Fees-Per Semester | |

Contd.

| Points to be answered | My facts |
|---|---|
| Course structure | |
| Internship details | |
| Major subjects | |
| Optional subjects | |
| Study hours per week | |
| Career outcome of the course. | |
| My career requirement. | |
| How course career outcome helps me to achieve my career outcome. | |
| Salary expected as beginner in Australia after completing the course. | |
| Salary expected in India after studies. | |
| Companies that would hire me in Australia or overseas. | |
| Companies that would hire me in India. | |
| Other colleges or university that I considered for admission. | |
| Reason I am choosing the particular institution for studies. | |
| Reason I am choosing Australia as study destination and not any other developed country or India. | |

## Criteria for checking you being a GENUINE student

A genuine student is a student with a good academic profile, enough IELTS score, clear future goal and one who has good knowledge about Australia and the course that he/she is going to study, and parents/ sponsor can afford his/her education.

**Table 44:** Criteria that makes you a genuine student.

| Criteria | Yes/ No/ Somewhat | Discuss with counselor |
|---|---|---|
| You know about the course content and course structure very well. | | |
| You know your career prospects and expected salary in India and around the world after completing the course. | | |
| You know exact expenses of your complete studies. | | |
| You have clear Return on Investment (ROI) plan (in terms of time and money both). | | |
| You have clear reasons of selecting Australia, and you are aware of different cities and the city chosen for studies. | | |
| You know about other universities offering the same program and reason for not going there. | | |
| You do not have long gap in studies of more than a year. | | |
| You have good IELTS score that satisfies the course requirement. | | |
| You have not chosen an irrelevant PR course e.g. choosing to go for Masters in Professional Accounting in Australia after having a B. Com degree with C grade or 40% marks in Maths and Accounts subjects. | | |
| You have not studied from a suspected OPEN school, from suspected boards or distant boards or fake universities (cross check list from UGC website). | | |

Contd.

| Criteria | Yes/ No/ Somewhat | Discuss with counselor |
|---|---|---|
| Your course duration is 2 years and you are aware of the student work permit requirements. | | |
| You have evidence of relationship with your sponsors. | | |
| If you are applying for diploma course, you know the progression route and work permit related conditions. | | |

## Criteria for checking a TEMPORARY student.

While the criterion of a genuine student is quite clear, it has been observed that most students get confused by the term temporary. It is important for students to know that the student visa is a temporary visa. This means that a student is expected to leave Australia after the completion of the studies. So when a student applies for admission or visa to study in Australia, it is expected that the student's intention is only to study in Australia. It is important for students to know that studying in Australia is also beneficial to their career growth outside Australia including their home country. Further, since study in Australia is expensive, they see it as an investment for their better future.

The international students are given work permits during and after studies, if a student wishes to gain local work experience. However, when a student is considering studying in Australia, it is expected that the immediate goal of the student is primarily the studies. The students should not be financially relying on earning money through part time work to sponsor their studies. This thinking and planning spoils the intention of the student visa. In order to be a GTE, it is critical to understand what and who is not a GTE.

**Table 45:** Check your chances of falling in the NOT temporary category.

| Details | Yes/ No/ Somewhat | Discuss particulars with Counselor |
|---|---|---|
| No/ Limited career growth in India after studying the chosen course from Australia. | | |

Contd.

| Details | Yes/ No/ Somewhat | Discuss particulars with Counselor |
|---|---|---|
| Education loan–guarantor is not parents and does not have sufficient relationship. | | |
| Income of the family is very low, less than 6 lakhs per year. | | |
| Low financial status in India–e.g. father is retired and family has 5 kids, no other source of income and ready to spend all retirement money on one child. | | |
| Irrelevant course or PR focused course without sufficient background (professional cookery, community health or professional accounting). | | |
| You have selected relevant course but PR focused (You have good marks in the same or related subjects from India but you are not sure about being successful in the course). | | |
| If married, your wife is going to study and your qualifications are poor. | | |
| If you have kids and do not have enough money and have taken a lot of sponsorships from different relatives. | | |
| Your sponsorship is uncertain–distant uncle or family friend is sponsoring who has limited income and investments and also has lot of personal responsibilities. | | |
| You have not studied from suspected OPEN school, from suspected boards or distant boards or fake universities (cross check list from UGC website). | | |

## What can you do to reassure GTE criteria?

1. Explore your career scope, when you return to India after completing the course from Australia.
2. Note down your potential salary after having the qualification from Australia. Also mention this in your SOP to show your awareness.
3. Be clear if your qualification from Australia is worth spending your money and time in Australia.

---

Refer Further Information Section/ Reference for website links from page 225–229.
You are recommended to study the appropriate material beforehand for information assessment.

## 23

# Immigration History

Apart from your application forms, GTE facts and other official requirement, one thing that can affect your visa is your immigration history. It is important that you record your previous international visa and travelling history accurately.You must provide your previous visa application information in your visa application irrespective of how old it is. Ignorance will be considered as a lie.

Sharing some categories below for clarity. You must fill in details as requested in the visa form:

1. If your visa has been rejected for Australia under same or any other visa category including visitor visa.
2. If you have been a minor applicant in any visa application when your parents applied for visa.
3. Your visa application to any other country apart from Australia to study, visit or migrate.

Your application will be assessed against the information provided on previous migration history and it will raise questions for further assessment. As a student you must be aware that the embassy has records of the visa applications and they will know about your visa history without you informing them. Your previous visa and travel history provides extra information about your profile and it has possibility to work in your favour if you handle the reasons well. If you lie about your immigration history, it will go against your profile.

**Table 46:** Collect data about your previous immigration history.

| Visa category Visitor/ Study/ Work/ Immigration | Visa status Approved/ Rejected | Visa issuance date | Evidence available Rejection letter/ visa label | Comments |
|---|---|---|---|---|
| | | | | |
| | | | | |

# 24
# Information Verification

The verification of the information provided in your application is one of the elementary requirements of the admission and visa processes. The universities and embassy have access to their own data and methodology to verify the information that you have provided. However it speeds up the processing if you provide correct contact details for verification of the documents that you believe will not have online verification access.

Your academics, IELTS and experience letters are verified along with the income tax returns, education loan letter and the financial particulars provided in the application. In order to expedite the visa verification process, you should inform your bank or the relevant authorities that they should expect a verification request from the embassy or the university and should respond to the query in a timely manner. You should provide complete address and contact details (including land line numbers) in your documents specially experience letters.

You do not need to verify your academic documents or the IELTS score. Most universities and embassy have access to verify this information at their end.

**Table 47:** Collecting contact details for verification.

| Authority | Contact Details |
|---|---|
| Employer/s | |
| The bank providing me the education loan. | |
| The banks having my sponsors investments and accounts | |

# 25

# Visa Interview

For the Australian student visa, personal or telephonic interview is not mandatory. However, a student may be called for an interview if something is not clear in the visa application. An interview is done to assess your preparation to study in Australia.

During the interview, it is expected that you are fully aware about your course and the living requirements in Australia along with your reasons for going to study in Australia. You may also need to demonstrate that you are capable to complete your study successfully and have arranged enough money to support your tuition, OSHC and living expenses in Australia.

Getting an interview call may also mean that the visa officer is not sure whether to reject or approve your case without speaking to you. In this case, it is an opportunity for you to convey your intention and provide complete information about yourself. Please note that it is your performance in the interview that will impact the final outcome of your application.

**A few points that may help you in your preparation for the interview are given below:**

1. Listen to the complete question before answering the visa officer.
2. Be precise and accurate in your answers.

3. The visa officer is not checking your accent, so don't be overly conscious of your English skills.
4. A visa officer just wants to know how truthful and logical you are in selecting your options to study in Australia, so be honest about it.
5. If an interview call is received in a market area, quickly go to a quiet place to give the interview. A noisy place will distract you. Be prepared for this situation and do not panic.
6. If you do not know something, simply admit it. Do not lie or make up a story. Don't try to over explain or confuse things while talking to the visa officer.
7. Prepare for the interview in advance as you may receive the interview call any time after submitting your visa application.
8. Understand the visa officer's question first and then give your answer. If you do not understand the question because of phone connectivity issue, ask the officer to repeat the question. Do not answer without understanding the question.
9. Give your personal reasons for the questions asked.
10. For career growth, work out options for both short-term and long-term career goals.
11. If visa officer repeats your answers to check other aspects—understand the statements first and then give answers—take a pause or break if needed. Spend a few seconds on thinking and then answer.
12. Visa interview is same as job interview—as long as you are well prepared, there is nothing to be worried about.

The following table gives some common questions asked during an interview. You can answer these to check your preparation for the interview.

**Table 48:** Questions to prepare for the visa interview.

| Questions | Your answers |
|---|---|
| Why have you chosen Australia as your study destination? | |
| Why have you chosen this particular course? | |
| Why have chosen this particular university? | |
| What are your career plans after completion of the course? | |
| Who motivated you to take up this course? | |
| Which other university or college offers this course? | |
| Why you are not studying the same course in India? | |
| Give a brief of your family background? | |

It is recommended that you be well prepared for the answers to the above questions. Take help from the interview in the admission section. Do not rehearse or memorize the answers. Put in effort to understand the question and the reason behind asking that question. It is a myth that the visa officer calls you to reject your case. In reality, a visa officer calls to check the integrity of the visa application submitted for processing.

# 26

# Visa Rejection

A visa rejection, though not wanted, may happen to any student who is not fully prepared. Therefore, it is very important that you understand its reasons before getting one. An awareness can help you to address the visa concerns efficiently. This chapter provides you with an overview and structure of a typical rejection letter. This data has been taken from a student rejection letter.

**A typical rejection letter has five sections:**

1. The applicant's claims
2. Information and evidence considered
3. Findings
4. Reasons
5. Decision

**Common reasons for the visa rejection may include:**

1. Inadequate or incorrect information provided.
2. Insufficient funds shown or embassy does not believe that the funds given in the visa file will be truly available to student at the time of need.

3. Lack of awareness about the future career prospects and return of investment.
4. Not performed well in the visa interview.
5. Fraudulent information provided.

   A sample refusal letter is given in the Appendix.

**Table 49:** Things you can discuss with your counselor to avoid visa rejection.

| Criterion | Question/ Notes to discuss with Counselor |
|---|---|
| Student's circumstances in their home country | |
| Student's potential circumstances in Australia | |
| Value of the course to the student's future | |
| Student's immigration history | |

# 27

# Application for your Spouse

Going for studies after marriage is possible and brings several advantages, such as married students feel less lonely as they have known company from the beginning. A spouse can help a student to manage work, home and studies. Also, spouse of a student studying a Master's degree is allowed to work full time in Australia and that supports the student financially. Being married, however, also adds more responsibility towards student's visa application. Therefore, it is important that you are aware of the conditions and relevant requirements for making application for your spouse.

Your visa application has two different applicants instead of one as in case of unmarried applicants. Additionally, you need to ensure that you have arranged enough money for the spouse's living expenses and health insurance. Your spouse's career growth and GTE requirement is an important aspect of your visa application.

## Spouse Profile Assessment

Your spouse's profile is equally important as your profile. A spouse is offered extra advantages like part time or full time work permit depending upon student's level of studies.

While assessing spouse profile, most important aspects that are taken into consideration are:

a. A genuine marriage.
b. The career prospects of the couple are balanced and appropriate.
c. Higher education of the student is more important than that of the spouse.
d. If wife is going for higher studies, husband's career is well settled already or he does not need further studies.
e. The spouse and student are both GTE.

## A Genuine Marriage:

In order to judge authenticity of the student's marriage, there are some criteria on the basis of which authenticity of the marriage is assessed. In order to assess the risk, the visa officer looks for the following:

- ✓ If the marriage is very recent and there is not enough proof of marriage available.
- ✓ If the couple is married very young (as compared to the normal local marriage standards).
- ✓ If wife is going to study when husband is less qualified—reasons for such a decision.
- ✓ If the marriage registration certificate is genuine.
- ✓ Whether the marriage photographs are original.
- ✓ If wife is going for studies, who is the sponsor—her father, husband or husband's family?

## Proof of your marriage

While you may wonder why you should need to prove your marriage authenticity to the visa officer, you would be surprised to know there is a proportion of applications where marital status is not found genuine and is manipulated for visa purposes only. It is because of this that all marriages need to prove their authenticity and provide genuine proofs.

Not all forms of evidence for marriages are considered sufficient. The case officer may place more weightage on some forms of evidence than the others. Some details are given below for your understanding. Please use them as reference guide only and provide as many strong and good proofs as possible.

**Strong evidence:** These include the documents that show joint assets, liabilities, undertakings, bequests etc. Some of them may include:

- ✓ Jointly owned assets such as real estate.
- ✓ Joint liabilities such as mortgages.
- ✓ Any joint undertakings such as a joint lease.
- ✓ Naming each other as beneficiaries in your respective wills or insurance policies.
- ✓ Child or children from the relationship.

**Good evidence:** These documents are generated by third parties that are addressed to student and spouse.

- ✓ Marriage Certificate
- ✓ Bank statements
- ✓ Bills, invoices, receipts in joint names
- ✓ Marriage photos—all ceremonies

**Decent forms of evidence:**The student or the spouse can directly generate this evidence, such as:

- ✓ Social media interaction with each other, e.g. face book marriage declaration or marital status on social media.
- ✓ Flight tickets or receipts showing your joint holidays or travels.
- ✓ Letters, invitations from social events.

**If necessary (normally provided on request of the visa officer):**

- ☺ Emails/letters to each other
- ☺ Records of telephone conversations

Not all proofs are required. However, proofs linked to genuine partnership in marriage would be expected according to the duration of marriage.

## The Spouse GTE Assessment

Like student, the spouse must also qualify the GTE requirement of being a Genuine and Temporary Entrant. For general requirements of GTE refer to the GTE section. Additionally, spouse cases also need to answer a few critical questions. These include:

1. As couple, whose career is more important and who is the prime earning member of the family?
2. If husband is class XII and wife is going to study Master's degree in Australia, what are the career prospects of the husband and why husband is not going to study when he is much less qualified?

## A Genuine Sponsor for Spouse

Since married students have the advantage of having two families to support their studies abroad, it is expected that the sponsorship is genuine and fair. The cases that invite additional scrutiny and doubt in the visa application are:

a. Recent marriage, with all expenses borne by wife's family.

b. Husband is going to study in Australia, and wife's family provides all sponsorship.

c. Wife's parents have other children, yet they are showing all of their money for their married daughter or her husband's education.

d. Wife is going to study a second Master's degree sponsored by her parents whereas husband has done class XII and does not have any good skills required for a career.

e. Husband does not have any high qualification; yet husband's parents are sponsoring their daughter-in-law for a Master's degree instead of educating their son.

## Case Studies

This section provides case studies that are meant to provide you with some insights for spouse cases. Use it only as reference guide.

### Case 1:

**Background:**

- Marriage is 6 months' old.
- Wife's qualification: 10th- 55%, 12th - 60%, B.Sc. (IT): 62%
- Husband's qualification: 10th: 60%, 12th: 55%, B. Com: 57%, passing year 2012, IELTS 6.0 overall with no bands less than 5.0. Since 2012 he is running a shop and filing ITRS of 4.5 lacs per year.

- Both live together in Yamuna Nagar, Haryana.
- Marriage certificate and photos available.
- Husband's father is running a shoe shop in the same area, selling shoes from a very long time with an annual income of 10 lacs per year and he has 3 other members to support in India.
- He will be sponsoring the couple with his fixed deposit of approximately 25 lacs.
- He is ready to take education loan on property and be a guarantor for the student.
- Student has saving of 5-6 lacs.
- Wife's family is not sponsoring.

**Ambition:** Husband wants to study MBA in Australia.

**Assessment:** Although the marriage is recent, the main earning member wishes to improve his skills and he has own money plus father's proper support to ensure he has enough money to complete his education. Wife is qualified and may find suitable work in Australia while husband focuses on studies.

## Case 2:

**Background:**

- Marriage is 4 years old.
- 1 child 2 years of age.
- Wife's qualification: 10th-65%, 12th: 68%, B.Sc. (Bio medical): 65%, IELTS 6.5 overall with no bands less than 5.5. She is working with a pharma company and taking salary in her account.
- Husband's qualification: 10th: 60%, 12th: 55%, B. Tech. (Civil): 57%, passing year 2013. Since then he is involved in the family business of building and construction company where he is supplying hardware like cement and steel. He is also taking construction projects. Business proofs are available. ITR filing: 10 lacs
- Younger brother is also involved in the business. He is married but does not have kids.

- Husband and his father will be sponsoring wife's studies in Australia. Husband has savings of around 8-9 lacs and father is providing fixed deposits of Rs 20 lacs plus supporting the education loan.
- Wife has personal saving of 3 lacs in her bank account.
- Wife's sibling who is working and not married will be sponsoring another 6 lacs. He files ITR of 8 lacs per year.

**Ambition:** Wife wants to study MBA (Healthcare Management). Child and husband plan to visit on dependent visa. Husband also has plans to enroll in some part time course related to his field and his business will be looked after by his brother and father during his absence. He will also work on his business expansion during his stay in Australia.

**Assessment:** Although wife wants to improve her career and she is not the prime earning member, the case still looks genuine as overall there is supportive environment for her education. Her ambition is clear; she has husband's support who is doing well financially plus she has other family members who are capable of giving her funds when she needs them.

## Case 3:

**Background:**

- Marriage is 1-year-old.
- Wife's qualification: 10th- 55%, 12th: 60%, B.Sc. (IT): 62%, IELTS 6.0 overall with no bands less than 5.0 (Reading and writing).
- Husband's qualification: 10th: 60%, 12th: 55%, (passed in 2012). Since then he is into dairy business of cows and cattle. He has dairy income certificate of around 3 lacs.
- He has two more brothers who are not married; one of them is studying and other is helping the father who has a tailoring shop.
- Husband's father will be sponsoring with bank statement of 10 lacs and one fixed deposit of 3 lacs.
- Husband has 2 lacs in his saving account.

**Ambition:** Wife wants to study Masters in IT and husband is looking forward to working during her studies.

**Assessment:** This case does not look like a GTE:

1. There is not enough financial preparation towards the money required for studies and living expenses.
2. Poor financial preparation makes them dependent on part time work earning in Australia.
3. Husband's English and work skills are not good enough to get skilled work in Australia.
4. Husband does not have qualification to be employed well in India or in Australia. Husband being the prime earning member should improve his studies and skills for better financial career.
5. Wife has enough skills to get a good job in India already.

The following table gives you the opportunity to fill details for your spouse and discuss it your counselor for visa purpose.

**Table 50:** Fill in the details to check spouse GTE.

| Criterion | Details / Notes to discuss with Counselor |
|---|---|
| Marriage is...... years old? | |
| Proof of marriage available | |
| Spouse qualification? | |
| Family liabilities? | |
| Spouse ambition? | |
| What is future planning of the family? | |
| As couple, whose career is more important for studying in Australia? | |

Contd.

| Criterion | Details / Notes to discuss with Counselor |
|---|---|
| Since living expenses are high for couple, who is sponsoring the spouse? | |
| Will the sponsor be able to give the required finances when needed by the couple? | |
| How much money each sponsor can give to the couple? | |

---

Refer Further Information Section/ Reference for website links from page 225–229.
You are recommended to study the appropriate material beforehand for information assessment.

Moving to Australia?
If you're ready to move, Australia's first bank is ready to welcome you.
Westpac Welcome
200
200 years proudly supporting Australia
ac Banking Corporation ABN 33 007 457 141 AFSL and Australian credit licence 233714.
WBC 00561 0

# SECTION 4

## Your Preparation Before Travel

# 28
# Travel

You need to do sufficient preparation for a peaceful journey to Australia. You should start your travel arrangements much before your visa approval. Tickets usually cost less when you book them early. Further, to avoid the last-minute rush to confirm your ticket close to the starting date of your course, it is essential to start this process at least 8 weeks in advance and start exploring options with airlines, agents or online.

While the advance bookings of the travel tickets saves money, you are not advised to purchase the full ticket unless your visa is received. If you do not receive your visa to travel on the booked ticket, you will lose the ticket money. As soon as your visa approval is acknowledged through email from the visa office, you must buy your ticket and send travel details to the person in Australia who is going to pick you up. You also need to ensure ticket and arrival confirmations before taking your flight.

To have a hassle-free journey, some things are very important to look after before travelling to Australia. You need to pack your luggage as per the guidelines to avoid going through the red line or taking something which is illegal.

**Hand Luggage:** You can carry the following items in your hand luggage so that they are handy and easy to find or show at the airport;

- Original Passport
- Visa Approval letter printout
- Academic documents and IELTS Score Card
- Offer letter from the college
- COE/s
- Address and phone number of the place where you will be staying in Australia.
- One set of clothes
- Doctor's prescriptions for medicines.
- A jacket because it is usually cold on the flight.
- Carry approximately 10 passport size photos.
- Travel Insurance
- A diary with contact details.

**Contact Details:** Do not just rely on your mobile. Take a small diary and note some critical contact details until you reach and are settled well in Australia. From India, you need to have the contact details of the following people:

- Parents
- Sibling
- Agent
- Friend/ someone close

From Australia, you need to have the following contact details:

- International Office of the University/College (details are also available on offer letter)
- Accommodation Officer—Both address and phone number
- Airport pick up Office/Officer
- Friends or relative in Australia

**Travelling Instructions:** It is important to follow the travel instructions as they are based on the past experiences of unprepared students. Please tick if you have these:

- Make sure your tickets are confirmed (not waitlisted) before travel.
- Check if you need a transit visa, in case you have to halt in some other country before reaching Australia.
- Specify seat and food choice in advance specially if you are a vegetarian (choose Indian vegetarian if not sure about the other options).
- Carry your passport and visa printout in safe pouch.
- Do not carry too much cash with you (Carry cash for 2-3 weeks' expenses and get the rest directly transferred into your bank account).
- Luggage guidelines—Ask travel agent and follow airline specifications.
- Carrying basic medicines—Make sure you have Dr's prescriptions.
- Put your perfumes in booked luggage. Perfumes and creams are not allowed in hand luggage.
- Carry original academic documents in hand luggage.
- Notarized photocopies in luggage—Carry a set of your academic documents notarized with the stamp of "VALID ABROAD" in your booked luggage.

## Airport Pick up

- Never underestimate the importance of someone picking you up when you reach the country for the first time. Arrange pick up in advance.
- If you do not know someone personally in Australia who can pick you up, take help of the institution. Most institutions have some kind of provision to arrange airport pick up.
- Always send your flight details at least 3 working days before the arrival date and take confirmation for your pick up.
- Make sure that you arrive on a weekday in working hours preferably. If that's not possible, ensure taking phone number of the person coming to pick you up and have the address ready where you are going to stay.
- Make sure you reach at least one day before the orientation date to cope with jet lag and adjust to the time difference.
- If you miss orientation with the institution's permission, keep one day for rest before enrolment.

**Table 51:** Your travel preparation

| Travel requirements | Yes/ No/ Yet to be done |
|---|---|
| Tickets confirmed | |
| Accommodation booked | |
| Airport pick up arranged | |
| Food in the flight confirmed | |
| Cash enough and kept safe | |
| Passport–original | |
| Visa–print out | |
| Travel insurance taken | |
| Important numbers noted | |
| Address noted | |
| COE and OSHC taken | |

Refer Further Information Section/ Reference for website links from page 225–229.
You are recommended to study the appropriate material beforehand for information assessment.

# 29
# Accommodation

Deciding where to stay and with whom to stay can be an intimidating experience especially if you do not know anyone in the country. To support the international students, universities and the local institutions offer a variety of accommodation opportunities. However, to get the right accommodation for yourself, you need to devote a fair amount time to explore the options. You need to start working on your accommodation when you receive your offer letter or have paid the tuition fees. You can go for the accommodation that suits your liking and budget. There are mainly four broad categories of accommodation for students in Australia. These include:

- On Campus
- Off Campus
- Homestay
- Sharing with other students
- Temporary Accommodation

**Table 52:** Your accomodation choices

| Categories | On Campus | Off Campus | Homestay | Sharing with other students | Temporary Accommodation |
|---|---|---|---|---|---|
| Ideal student category | Under Graduate/ Research students | Post Graduate Students | Students who need guardianship/ someone who likes to live with another family. | Recommended after first semester when student has own friends to share the accommodation with. | Post graduate students who get late in booking their accommodation or someone who is not sure what to choose until they reach Australia. |
| Duration –asked for booking by the providers | Usually 6-10 months of advance booking is required. | Usually 6-10 months of advance booking is required | Duration varies from 4 to 10 months. | Usually 6 months to a year. | From 6 to 12 weeks. |
| Sharing options availability | Personal, Twin or Multiple | Personal, Twin or Multiple | Usually one student per family. | Usually 3 to 4 people depending upon size of the apartment. | Personal, Twin or Multiple Sharing. |
| Cost | AUD 200–600 per week | AUD 200–600 per week | AUD 280–320 per week depending upon guardianship requirement. | AUD 150–400 per week depending upon size and location. | AUD 80–200/ night |
| Food optins | With/ without Food | With/ without Food | Usually with food providing breakfast and dinner. | Without food/ personal or shared cooking | With/ without Food |

It is highly recommended that the student and their family book the accommodation. It is very important that your accommodation suits your personal requirements including your food habits and personal allergies. The accommodation officers prefer that the students take charge of the booking and be aware of their requirements. Students can also chat online with their accommodation officer. Your agent will be able to help you in sharing the accommodation information and available options.

When you decide to book accommodation, ensure that you read instructions on the website carefully and ask questions about things which are not clear to you. Since you are planning to stay in a new environment, you are responsible for communicating all your requirements and inform appropriate authorities in advance or before the deadline if there is any. You must answer questions freely in the accommodation form, and do not hesitate to convey your preferences.

Unlike India, bedding may not include mattress and/or bed sheet because this is very personal to people in Australia. So you need to check the arrangements for bed sheets or any other similar thing that you need in your accommodation. Always check the list of the things that are provided and make a list of the things that you would need to buy. You may carry some things from India.

Food is a very important aspect to consider while booking accommodation. Look for vegetarian and halal options (if you need any of these). Assess your culinary skills and taste preferences before selecting an option of being catered. Have a look at the cuisines and menus (if available) before choosing accommodation with food. It is highly recommended to learn basic cooking before leaving India.

It is recommended to stay independent in the beginning and enter shared accommodation later with the known people and environment.

You must get the accommodation information early to avoid missing any booking deadline. A comfortable accommodation provides peace of mind.

**Table 53:** To choose your accommodation, answer these questions.

| Criteria | Comment |
|---|---|
| How intense is my course? | |
| Will I be able to focus on studies if I share accommodation? | |
| Can I adjust with the food provided by the college? | |
| Can I cook by myself? | |
| Am I confident to share accommodation with unknown students? | |
| What is the travel time to my institution? | |
| What are the booking deadlines for getting the accommodation of my choice? | |

You must visit the accommodation booking section on the university or college website as soon as you decide to confirm your admission at the institution of your choice. For more information, you can visit websites given in the *"Further Information Section"* and discuss it with your counsellor.

Refer Further Information Section/ Reference for website links from page 225–229.
You are recommended to study the appropriate material beforehand for information assessment.

# 30
# Food and Cooking

Australian food is very distinct and different from what we eat in India. In such a case, if you know cooking it can be very handy for you, particularly when you are not used to western tastes. Eating out on a regular basis could be expensive and may not be as satisfying as you would like it to be.

As a student you would be responsible for your studies, health and also work if you take a part time job. For successful studies, it is critical for you to keep yourself healthy. An unfamiliar food may cause allergies. Indian students are noted to develop some vitamin deficiency due to change in food habits. Therefore, it is very important that you schedule your food or cooking in order to be fit and healthy.

Most accommodation services also have options of providing cooked food, which can be one option for managing your regular meals. You can also look for the accommodation that can offer cuisine that is close to your taste buds and you would enjoy it on a daily basis. It is recommended that you learn basic cooking while you are in India. Most suburbs have Indian grocery shops and you can find almost all spices, vegetables and groceries that you can get in India. You can download google map on your mobile to find restaurants and shops in and around your area.

## Vegetarian Food

The meaning of vegetarian food differs in various parts of the world. For many countries, egg and fish are included in the vegetarian food. Therefore, it is important that you specify your requirements correctly and mention yourself as Indian vegetarian if travelling or eating out.

## Halal food

There is respect for people who have the choice of eating Halal food in Australia. You can ask this question without hesitation instead of not eating in a restaurant. Usually restaurants have the option of halal food if you want it.

# 31
# Communication

Communication with your family members is very important while you are away. It saves you from the pain of loneliness and also reduces stress for your family who are often terrified when you travel abroad for first time by yourself. You can communicate through various channels including phone, internet, post cards and so on.

## Phone

A phone call is the first thing you want to make as soon as your flight lands on the ground. Contacting your driver or friend who has come to pick you up from the airport is the immediate requisite. Most students and their families are anxious if this journey is student's first air travel alone. The long distance and time difference makes the situation quite worrisome for the family until you call back home and inform them that you have landed safely. You feel calm and confident if you have the phone at that time.

You will be using your mobile more than you have done in India. You will need it for your travel all the time. You will use it to check your bus routes and timings for college travel, finding location of your food joints & shopping etc. Your mobile will keep you mobile all the time.

You will need the following on your mobile on arrival:

- WhatsApp or any data calling app
- Google map
- Email Configuration
- Calendar & reminders
- Skype
- Music Apps

While it is possible that you are carrying your phone with yourself, you would need a local SIM or mobile plan to call India. It can be confusing when you are new in the country and do not have adequate knowledge. You will need a good calling plan. Remember, you will be homesick in the beginning and miss your friends and family until you make new friends on the campus. Having a plan with unlimited calling time value to your country is highly recommended. You may change the plan once you are settled. However, in the beginning you will need to be connected with people to discuss everything from food recipes to new ways of studying and assignments etc. It is critical that you have an activated SIM when your flight lands at the airport. The best time to buy a SIM is before leaving the country so that you can share mobile number with family in India and concerned people in Australia.

You can buy the SIM from the education agencies. You can also find this out from your counselor. Optus, Vodafone & Telstra are the main mobile service providers in Australia. It is important to consider basic, yet highly essential points at the time of buying the mobile connection:

- ✓ Signals accessibility
- ✓ Call and data charges
- ✓ Internet data quality
- ✓ Outlets accessibility
- ✓ Availability to buy in India
- ✓ Activation or deactivation process
- ✓ Customer support services

In order to start the calls, you simply need to call the customer care and they will do the job. If you want to change the service, you need to apply to the new provider and request for change.

Although it's easy to find Wi-Fi on campus and most of the accommodation places, you will still need good data in your mobile especially while you are travelling. You will need data to check bus routes and listen to online music etc. You will not want to get stuck in a lonely place without anyone knowing your whereabouts. While choosing your data provider, choose the one who has the best signals set up, is cost effective and provides excellent customer support.

In some cases, using calling cards can be cheaper. However, you need to check the calling cards prices and value individually. The quality of calls may not be same as you expect. Also, you may not get data on the calling cards.

**Table 54:** Plan for your communication means.

| Criteria | My Notes | Counselor Recommendation |
|---|---|---|
| Mobile Provider Name (which is suitable) | | |
| Calling Plan I need (Limited/ unlimited) | | |
| Data plan I need | | |
| Cost of the complete plan that I have chosen | | |
| Date of buying the SIM | | |
| Place of buying the SIM | | |
| Questions I need to ask from the counselor/ provider | | |
| Contact number of Mobile provider/ Customer service | | |

**Table 55:** List of the people and services for whom you need to save numbers.

| People & Services | ✓ They have saved my number | ✓ I have saved their number |
|---|---|---|
| Mother | | |
| Father | | |
| Siblings | | |
| Person picking me up from the airport. | | |
| Accommodation office | | |
| International office of the University or college | | |
| Agent's office in India | | |
| Friends in India | | |
| New friends made in Australia. | | |

## Laptop:

Your laptop is another necessity for both studies and communication. While buying your laptop or mobile, you need to look for:

- International warranty & servicing facilities
- Universal/ Australia specific Power Adaptor

**You are recommended to have the following installed in your laptop systems:**

- MS Office—licensed
- Outlook Configurations
- Skype
- Wi-Fi set up
- Other softwares needed for you to study your course
- Anti-Virus

You need to set up your laptop for your requirements of assignments, projects, internet, mailing and chatting with your friends. You should transfer data to your laptop that you would like to use in Australia and use it in India. It is important that you are familiar with your laptop and its functions. You are also recommended to do the same with your mobile. Ensure email setting and download some apps in advance along with your address book.

## Charger/ Adaptor

Electrical sockets (outlets) in Australia usually supply electricity at between 220 and 240 volts AC. Ensure compatibility at the time of purchase. Once you are sure of compatibility, you could simply buy an adaptor.

It is also highly recommended that you keep all your assets carefully and safely. Do not show off money—cash, expensive items like watches, laptops, mobile etc. As you are new to the place, if you lose any of these, even by mistake, it may be difficult to get it back and you may need to pay much more to buy it again.

32

# Clothing

Clothing is a very important aspect of your preparation for travelling to Australia. This is because Australia's weather conditions vary significantly from that of India. Although, shopping can be a very tempting option, it is highly recommended that you plan well for your clothing while you are in India. It is important to choose your clothes carefully considering local culture and lifestyle in Australia.

India has most of the top brands available in its market, so buying clothes according to different weather conditions is not very difficult. It is recommended that you plan your clothing for the next six months according to the weather condition of the city that you are going to visit. You can check the temperature and wind speed of most cities through Internet. Once you know the temperature, you can plan your clothing based on your dressing needs and style. Students usually wear smart casual clothes to college except for presentations and interviews which require formal official clothing. It is also recommended that you choose neutral colors which are not too bright or too fancy. Most places in Australia are cold, so it is better to consider layered clothing than buying heavy jackets.

**In general, you may require clothing for the following situations:**

- Smart casuals for attending classes.
- Clothes for entertainment or weekend fun.
- One set of formal clothes for appearing at presentations or interviews.
- An Indian traditional outfit for functions or cultural events.
- Sleepwear
- Undergarments & socks
- Accessories–scarves, caps and tie etc.

**It is recommended that you track the following:**

✓ Buy your clothes in advance and use them once in India.

✓ Learn to wash your clothes to avoid weeping colors in laundry or spoiling all your clothes as you would be washing most of them together in the washing machine.

✓ Learn to manage your clothes while washing and ironing.

✓ Keep your dry cleaning to minimum.

✓ Buy clothes, which are machine washable. Check labels.

✓ Do not buy too many clothes (you may find different fashions and styles and would like to buy them in Australia).

It may look strange to give so much importance to clothing but this is something which will save you from a lot of trouble if you learn how to take care of your clothes from your mothers. You may have a laundry facility, which is paid, and you would like to wash most of your clothes at one go. You may think that you have helped your mother in the past in washing which should be sufficient, but as you have no external support in Australia, learning about clothes, colours and washing requirements may help you to save your clothes from getting damaged in the machine.

**Table 56:** Washing for different clothes.

| Clothes Category | Machine wash | Hand wash |
|---|---|---|
| Jeans | | |
| White colors | | |
| Colorful Cottons | | |
| Winter wears | | |
| Any other | | |

**Note:** Do not indulge in too much shopping. Take things for the first 6 months and buy the rest in the country. Find out local sale dates and put them on your calendar. Most of the information is available online.

---

Refer Further Information Section/ Reference for website links from page 225–229.
You are recommended to study the appropriate material beforehand for information assessment.

# 33

# Skills Required

Most Indian students are used to living with their families where either parents or other family members manage the necessities of life. In this respect, living in Australia is very different, as students need to manage most of their work and necessities on their own. Managing yourself in this new country requires you to prepare yourself with a new set of skills. These are easy to develop if you are aware of them.

## Time Management

- You need to know that the day starts early in Australia. Select your time table carefully as per your sleep requirement.
- Be on time to select your course from the list, otherwise you will have a limited choice.
- Make your list of daily activities or priorities on paper, including both study and household work such as cleaning, making breakfast, getting ready and travelling time.
- Make sure that you have a daily, weekly and monthly schedule ready.

## Budget Management

- This is the most challenging part for majority of the students.
- List your daily, weekly and monthly requirements and their related expenses.

- List expenses for tuition fee, accommodation, electricity, mobile bill, grocery, travelling, books, entertainment and miscellaneous.

## Cooking Skills

- If you do not eat food of your choice, you will not feel happy and that may make you sick.
- Learn to cook your favorite food.
- Cook it at home in India for everyone a few times before travelling.
- Make a list of all Indian spices that you need as you can buy these in Australia. This also means that you don't need to carry them along with you.
- You can socialize very well if you know how to barbeque.
- List your weekly and monthly cooking schedules.
- List your weekly and monthly grocery shopping. Bulk Shopping is recommended as most accommodations have refrigerators.

## Dressing and Clothing

- Make sure that whatever clothes you are taking with yourself, you have already tried and tested in India at least once. Wash them before taking them. This will make you know whether the dress bleeds colour.
- You can also learn to dress up properly for occasions.
- Learn how to maintain different kinds of clothes.

## Health Management

- Make sure that you floss your teeth, wear clean clothes, have a proper haircut, cut your nails and use deodorants.
- Eat healthy food at regular times.
- Have enough sleep.
- Exercise regularly to avoid any weakness or disease.
- Understand the health insurance policy well.
- Ask for bulk (cashless) billing options from the health insurance provider for doctor's visit.

# 34

# Banking-Moving & Managing Money

As an imperative characteristic of studying in Australia, you will suddenly find yourself managing a lot of money for your studies and living expenses. Handling money may appear exciting but it has the potential to place student under pressure for its safety and management.

By now, you must be aware of your expenses on weekly, monthly, and quarterly basis. Make sure that you open a bank account as quickly as you can and travel with minimal cash. You may start budgeting and handling banking in India for your family to understand and practise it. Learn to handle money for a successful independent journey to Australia. Some of the details shared in this section are designed to help you prepare in advance.

**Australian banking landscape:**

Opening a bank account is a quick and easy process in Australia. What's important is that you must comprehend the terms and conditions of operating the bank account. Majority of the information is provided at the time of opening the account. Most of the banks have their mobile app and you can easily operate your account from your mobile.

**Things to know:**

1. You will operate your account through debit card or online.
2. You must know your debit card transaction limit.
3. Be aware of the transaction fees while using other banks' ATM machines.

**Initial mistakes made by the students:**

1. Carrying cash for a long time and being stressed for its safety.
2. Lending money to people without knowing them well.
3. Carrying too much cash all the time.

**Educate yourself with these facts**

**Can I open a bank account in Australia while I am still in India?**
Yes, there is a provision of opening a bank account from India.

**Can I transfer money in this bank account before leaving the country?**
Yes, you can transfer money in your account while you are still in India.

**Once I am in Australia, can my parents transfer money to me in the Australian account?**
Your parents can deposit money in your Australian account from India which you can access for your expenses in Australia.

**Can I give my Australian bank account details to my bank in India that has given me education loan for my studies and living expenses?**
Yes, you can share the details with your bank in India.

**How do I access my money in Australia?**
You need to visit the nearest bank branch with original passport and visa copy to get your account activated for withdrawing your money.

**Table 57:** Check your banking preparation

| Self-Check Questions | Yes/ No/ Comments |
|---|---|
| I have read the banking process and related terms and conditions applicable in Australia. | |
| I am aware of my monthly living expenses. | |
| I have shared my bank account details with my parents to transfer money in future towards my living expenses in Australia. | |
| I have shared my Australian bank account facts with the Indian bank (that has approved my education loan) to transfer my living expenses as requested. | |

# SECTION 5

## Your arrival & settling down in Australia

# 35

# Adapting to Cultural Differences

The Australian culture is very different from that of India, and the culture and social customs are hard to define. It is a highly multicultural country with people from more than 210 countries. To avoid any kind of cultural shock, it is important that you learn about the culture and people of Australia. There are various aspects of lifestyle and behavior that may not be familiar or natural to you. Some of these are discussed in the following paragraphs and may help you to prepare yourself in advance. It is important to understand the basic expectations in various areas of life to avoid unwanted situations from arising.

**Cleanliness and hygiene:** You will find that the people are clean and highly organized. You are also expected to manage basic hygiene and be organized. Few important points of basic hygiene are:

- Do not litter on the road.
- Keep your room/ home clean.
- Segregate biodegradable or non-biodegradable waste.
- Maintain personal hygiene—use a deodorant to remove body odour. Your clothes may not seem dirty but have body odour if not washed regularly. Maintain a proper haircut and shave regularly.

**Politeness:** People in Australia are very polite and expect you to be polite as well. This is also a necessity when the community is so diverse. In this context, you need to practice the following:

- Please and thank-you are very important to use wherever appropriate.
- Be polite and calm—people do not speak in high-pitched voices or too loudly.
- Politeness with the clerical staff and with general people is expected irrespective of their job profile including garbage collector, milkman or lady at the sales counter.

**Socializing:** In Australia, you will meet people from different nationalities who have different socio-cultural practices. Many Indian students tend to be around other Indian students, which is not encouraged. It is advisable that:

- You mingle and mix with people from different nationalities.
- You should also engage yourself in co-curricular, non- study and/or sports activities.
- You can also join a sports club on campus or off campus to socialize or find people of similar interest.

**Be Yourself:** Being understanding and cooperative does not mean that you shouldn't do what you like or force yourself to do everything that others tell you to do. It is all right to say 'no', if you think you cannot manage something. It is recommended that you have basic knowledge of India and Australia to participate fully in the discussions.

**Money:** Money is very important for you in Australia. Almost all the services are paid activities. So, it is important that you save your money and do not waste it. It is also advised that:

- You don't ever borrow money from anybody or lend money to anyone.
- You can use second hand shops for buying books.
- You always read the terms and conditions given behind every product including accommodation contracts.

**Health:** As you are exposed to very different food habits and lifestyle in Australia, it is important that you manage your health. It is advisable that:

- You keep a careful check on your health.

- Eat Healthy—organize your food menu.
- Exercise daily.
- Learning to swim is recommended.

## Important Do's and Don'ts List

✓ Have knowledge about what is legal and what is illegal.

✓ Follow rules strictly—do not fall into the trap of finding loopholes.

✓ Listen to the person carefully who advises you to change your college in Australia as most likely the person will benefit from this act of yours. You must evaluate the suggestions given by the people carefully before acting. You should continue sharing your life with the family or take professionals advice if needed.

✓ Collect flyers at station/airports to keep yourself updated.

✓ Avoid unwanted counseling from friends and unknown people.

✓ Avoid going to casinos.

✓ Budget money. Plan monthly and weekly budget in the initial stages.

✓ Learn to travel in the metro. Have some basic knowledge.

✓ Learn to use maps including Google map.

✓ Sniffing and honking horns is considered rude.

✓ Create habit of using dustbins.

✓ Learn about filling forms at airport/ disembarkation.

✓ Say yes if you are interested, you may not be offered the chance again.

✓ Learn to do your work by yourself; no maids or servants are available.

✓ You can buy a second hand car. Follow the rules about driving licenses.

✓ If you are going in a group, you can always go Dutch (sharing of bill—it can be divided by the number of people).

✓ Shopping once a week is suggested.

✓ Practice computer skills for MS Office. You will need to do assignments on computer.

✓ Teach your parents how to communicate through Skype or WhatsApp etc.

✓ Identify location of nearby bank.

- ✓ Carry a pressure cooker.
- ✓ Learn about what to do in case of loss of passport—where to go and what to do, create basic knowledge about it.
- ✓ Read about your insurance claim procedure in advance.
- ✓ Be aware of cashless facilities for single/bulk billing.
- ✓ Carry spectacles/lenses, or both.
- ✓ Dental work is very expensive and normal insurances do not cover dental procedures.
- ✓ Get your eye test done before leaving India.
- ✓ A lot of work is done by the international office, so be aware of its location and services provided.
- ✓ If you are taking accommodation, you must be aware of the bond requirement.
- ✓ Property dealers do not charge fees.
- ✓ Property dealer's inspection is exhaustive and you are expected to maintain the property well.
- ✓ Create knowledge about opening of a bank account.
- ✓ Don't wander around late at night.
- ✓ Try and be in a group while travelling.
- ✓ Don't do jobs, which locals don't do.
- ✓ Don't do late night jobs.
- ✓ Try and avoid lonely places.
- ✓ Take a job where you get paid with TFN (Tax File Number).
- ✓ Students need Tax File Number for part time job salary payment.
- ✓ Carry college ID cards.
- ✓ Lecturers are called by their first name.
- ✓ Learn toilet manners.
- ✓ Spitting is not allowed.
- ✓ There are penalties for littering.

# 36

# Managing Studies

As your primary purpose to go to Australia is to study, managing your studies must remain a priority for you. This means you need to manage everything else in such a manner that you do not compromise on your studies. There are various support services available at the university that you can use for your benefit.

**Orientation:** Your University organizes the orientation for you to get to know your campus. This is the very first step towards knowing about your university, library and all the other services that you will need to use. This is also an opportunity to make new friends, so make sure that you participate fully in the orientation program. You are highly recommended to read the orientation details on the institution's website and prepare for it. To get maximum benefit, you need to ask questions wherever you have a doubt. You should not feel shy as participation is more important that winning any game in Australia.

If you miss orientation, or do not attend the program fully due to any reason, then you can get more information and support from:

- International office of the institution.
- Student Support center of the institution.

**Instructions:** As you are treated as an adult, no one will give you instructions on how to study or work. This is a cultural difference between India and Australia. So, you are unlikely to receive multiple instructions or reminders for rules or the deadlines. It is highly recommended that you keep all instructions given to you as per the course guideline at one place and put an alarm for the reminder.

Integrity is highly valued in Australia, and therefore they expect you to do everything on time. Also, people in Australia may not look serious or speak in a serious tone, but that doesn't mean that you will not face setbacks for your lack of integrity. Breaking any rule, deadline, instruction, or recommendation may have serious consequences.

**Time-table:** You are expected to follow all the guidelines and submit your assignments on time. It is very important that you make a timetable for yourself. It is also recommended that you keep it handy, so that you can access it anytime and check it every day.

**Copying or Plagiarism:** Copying data for your assignment or project is a punishable offence in Australia. If you copy data from the Internet and do not provide reference, you will fail in the course. Ignorance is not accepted. There are now softwares available that can find the source of your copied data and it is easy to catch if you have copied your assignment.

**Attendance Requirement:** Your attendance is important and is counted towards your final scores. You should, therefore, count your attendance on a regular basis to avoid any last moment issues.

**Warning or reminders:** Contrary to your expectation, you may find that no one is questioning or reminding you about your project deadlines. This is because you will be given all your deadlines and guidelines at the beginning of the course. You are treated as an adult and if you fail to meet any deadlines, you may be asked to pay the penalty without any further discussion. This applies to almost all situations that embrace deadlines. You are yourself responsible for managing your time and reminders about your deadlines.

## Major differences

- No one will ask you to do anything. You are expected to look after yourself, your studies and work both.
- You are treated as an adult who alone is responsible for his/her actions.
- You can get help, but only if you ask.
- Your privacy is important and your parents will get your results only if you give a written consent to your institution, else university will not give information about your performance to anyone, including your parents.

## Recommendation:

✓ Organize your room well. Have a big calendar. You can carry it from India. Put all-important dates and mark them where you can see everything all the time.

✓ Set reminders for important dates and activities in advance so that you are reminded well before the deadlines. Put these reminders also in your mobile and laptop both.

✓ Take some posters which inspire you and keep you focused.

✓ Have your long-term goal written in front of you.

✓ Be focused on "REASONS OF COMING TO AUSTRALIA."

✓ Do not do things which you are not sure of.

---

Refer Further Information Section/ Reference for website links from page 225–229.
You are recommended to study the appropriate material beforehand for information assessment.

# 37

# Ways of Managing Money

It is very important that you save money in Australia as things are expensive and you have a very limited budget. For this you need to inculcate the habit of saving and avoiding unnecessary expenses on not so important things. You can also save money by using student discounts.

**Student Discounts:** International students get discounts in many places including:

a. Shopping

b. Theatre

c. Dinning & Take Away

d. Theme parks & Attractions

You should check with the international office at your institution and follow the process to get the student discounts. You may also be entitled for student discount for buying laptops and mobiles. Always ask for student discount from the shops to ensure that you are not paying more money than you should. You should carry your international student identity card or university card to get access to the discounts available in a restaurant, movie theatre and for shopping etc.

**Part time work:** Part time work can be another way to increase your budget and save money. Working part time not just provides pocket money but also offers a great opportunity to interact with local people, learn about their culture and make new friends. While part time work provides huge opportunities to students, it has potential to damage studies and health if it is not handled properly.

Ensure you have settled well with your studies, sleep, food and time before exploring part time work. On an average, it takes a couple of months to settle and understand the pattern of your study timetable including projects and assignments. Remember if you fail in a subject, you would need to pay to repeat and that will increase your time and expenses both.

It is important that you write down your reasons to work part time before starting it. **Your reasons may include:**

- Exposure to the local culture.
- Practicing and learning the local language.
- To earn pocket money.
- Internship—enhancing the outcome of the program by practicing it.
- Work experience related to your qualification.

Once you have noted your reason to work part time, you can find a suitable job that matches your choice at multiple places. Finding part time work can happen anywhere and anytime. You should keep sharing your interest and resume with relevant authorities including:

- Career services facility provided by your institution.
- Visit individual websites of the companies to find out relevant work.
- Distribute your CVs at individual shops.
- Register yourself with job websites; they also have details of part time job vacancies.

Most of the organizations provide positions which are part time and suitable for international students, particularly if you have some skills like software development or coffee making with professional coffee machines. **Some of the popular places for getting part time jobs are:**

- Campus—student union, library, canteen or international office. Keep checking notice boards and newsletters on your portal.

- Restaurants, hotels and takeaways food joints.
- Departmental stores of all sizes from small to big ones including Coles and Woolworths.
- Petrol Pumps—quite flexible timings.
- Clothing and electronic shops looking for sales executives.
- Coffee shops—it is worth learning making coffee with professional coffee machines.
- Cinema and game studios—techie students have fun selling games to kids.

While all these jobs are fun to do, and provide you with exposure and money, nothing replaces the power of skilled internship related to your studies. You should remain focused on getting a place to practice what you study at the institution. You may also find that many jobs related to your studies are voluntary and not paid but provide huge opportunity to work with professional organizations in skilled areas. Voluntary work provides huge platform for experience and it is highly recommended to find such work if you get the opportunity. Voluntary work usually varies from four to twelve weeks. This is not mandatory but it has huge potential to put you in contact with your future organization, which has the potential to hire you on completion of studies.

There are a few individual characteristics that can help you in finding work of your choice. In big cities, there is competition for good work. You need to stand out interested and capable to get the work. Apart from your visa and time availability, other things that influence this are:

- Enthusiasm and interest.
- Grooming and etiquette.
- Commitment.

Once you have finalized the part time work of your choice, you need to do a few important things:

1. Open a bank account in an Australian Bank.
2. Get your TFN number online before starting to work.
3. Have a simple resume ready with your skills, English ability and work rights.

Besides, there are some precautions that you need to take before starting your part time work.

- Do not start focusing on work before settling down in your studies.
- Do not ever work for cash (you will be paid very less and it will not be worth spending your time. Above all it is illegal and you may get into serious trouble).

# 38

# Managing Emotions

For most students, going to Australia for study can be the first-time experience of going out and living without family support in an entirely foreign environment. Students experience various emotions that they are not used to and do not know how to handle. This chapter can help you to be aware of them and become prepared to handle them with ease.

## Homesickness

Homesickness is natural as every student misses his/her family and friends. It happens to almost every child, adult or even family. The good thing about homesickness is that it is very easy to deal with in today's world of communication. A few things you need to take care of are:

1. **Set up a communication channel with your family:** It is important that you set up a communication channel to talk to your family while you are in India. You should train both your mother and father on how to use Skype, WhatsApp or any other data-calling channel. Best practice is to use these services while you are in India a few times, so that it is easy to do it from Australia
2. **Understand time difference & share your study timetable with family:** It is important that you and your family are aware of the

time difference and know about your study and work schedule, so that you do not miss their call. Also, practice sharing your experiences with family as it helps to reduce your homesickness. The communication will be most important in the first three months and gradually you and your family will be used to the new situation.

3. **Sleep well & organize your food in advance:** Eating right and sleeping on time will benefit both your health as well as studies. Do not try to get everything done as soon as you arrive in Australia. If you keep yourself healthy and fit, you will be able to achieve more.

4. **International Student Support Centre:** Each institution has an International student support center, which is focused on international students' welfare. You need to understand how to use their services and not be shy in asking questions. Take your other friends there as well. Communication is the key to address homesickness. Sometimes calling people back in India may exaggerate your problem. In this situation, it is best to bring your issues to the attention of the international office, which is solely meant for supporting and guiding international students. Always check with the college authorities before following friends' advice instinctively as in some situations they are in a better position to help than your friends.

5. **Be ready to make new friends & keep your self-esteem high:** In a new place, you may find that people are very different in looks, behavior, food and dressing style. The good thing about Australia is that the people appreciate differences. No one minds your appearance if you look different or you are new to the place trying to find your way. Look for what's good there and learn from the new culture and people. However, being new may put you in some situations where you would not know what to say or what to do. Remember this happens to everyone who travels to a new place including the smartest student of the institution. All you need to do is to learn from your early mistakes, improve, and keep your self-esteem high. Very soon, you will start enjoying your new environment, friends and classmates.

## Distractions

In Australia, the environment is open and the students have the freedom of not being questioned by families for their actions and activities, which may also tempt you to get involved in drinking and night outs. While you are free to do that, it is important that you remember your basic aim for being in Australia is your studies. So, you should ideally avoid any distraction that will keep you away from your goal. Some of the common distractions and the ways to deal with them are as follows:

**Distraction 1: Late night parties**

**Way to respond:** If you have to attend then make sure that you know the people well with whom you are going to party. It is also important that you know and have planned for your next day academic schedule. You should also avoid drinking and driving to reach home safely.

**Distraction 2: Unwanted counseling for easy way out**

**Way to Respond:** You will get a lot of suggestions from old students, peers, local agents and immigration agents who may also have genuine advice to offer. Some suggestions may appear very attractive in short-term. Make sure that you use the right channels to cross check the information. People may suggest ways to settle fast in Australia. Be aware that there is no short cut to success and if you use any loopholes in the system, your long-term goal may get adversely affected.

**Distraction 3: Excessive part time work or cash jobs**

**Way to Respond:** Many students are lured to extremely low paid, part time jobs, which are illegal and they are paid in cash. This affects student health, studies, visa and overall prospects. It is the student's responsibility to say no to this kinds of job and manage their time and budget well.

**Distraction 4: Attraction towards opposite sex**

**Way to Respond:** While it is natural to get attracted towards the opposite sex, it is important that you understand the cultural differences first, and be responsible for your behavior. This can affect your studies as well, which is your primary aim in Australia.

**Distraction 5: Drugs**

**Way to Respond:** This one is very easy to handle. You just need to use your common sense and say "NO", no matter how curious you are and how much your friends insist. This must be a complete NO.

**Distraction 6: Alcohol**

**Way to Respond:** Students associate alcohol with status symbol but it is not. You will learn slowly that people are respected for their values. People drink with a lot of grace and dignity without losing control over themselves. If you do not drink, they do not mind it at all. You can join the party and drink anything else which is non-alcoholic.

## Unmet Expectations

As Australia would be very new to you, it is possible that you may find some things that happen to you very disappointing. Most of such issues are emotional rather than physical. It is possible that you feel one of the following:

- It is not as great a place as I thought it would be.
- Is it worth having come so far to study?
- Why did I come here?

Many of these feelings erupt when one is away from the home environment. It is important that you recognize these as emotional reactions rather than as actual problems. This is because you chose Australia for a better future, which it still provides, but you do not like the journey, as it gets tough at times, particularly in the beginning when you don't have many friends and you feel alone. In such a situation, it is important that you always discuss concerns with the right person at the university or at home. It is hard to enjoy the college from the very first day itself. This happens even to students who join a new college in India.

You may find things different from India and you will have questions popping up as part of the cultural shock. Every student thinks that his problem is personal and does not go to the right person for help. You need to accept the fact that the culture is different and as you start to understand that you will find the people to be very friendly, frank, helpful and straightforward.

Sometimes, the institution's team members are unable to do something for you if you have by passed the rules. The rules are strict and apply to everyone. You need to learn to listen and follow rules carefully. You are expected to be independent to take care of yourself. If you need help, say exactly what help you need to the concerned person.

# 39

# Migration Pathways after Completing your Studies in Australia

The migration pathway section is created to help students get a basic understanding of the process of migration to Australia. As a student, you need not get into the details at this stage. However, you should be aware of the impact of your higher studies on your settlement should you decide to pursue it in the future.

We are thankful to Mr Ashwin Tyagi, who has studied migration law at Australian National University and is also a graduate in business from Cornell-RMIT. Mr Tyagi has over 15 years of experience in international recruitment, management and Immigration services industry in Australia. He is a Registered Migration Agent (MARN: 1575846), a member of the Migration Institute of Australia (MIA) and Principal RMA at Immigration Hotspot Australia.

The Australian government provides benefits to the students who want to settle after their studies by giving them extra points towards their application for residency. This means that you can benefit from this opportunity by completing your studies in time. There are, however, some myths about migration and its connection with student visa. To be successful at both studies and migration, it is important to understand the purpose of each visa individually.

**Some of the common myths are:**

- I must take a course that is listed on the Medium and Long-term Strategic Skills List (MLTSSL), although I do not like the course and I have failed in that course in India.
- I can take up any course and change that in Australia as soon as I arrive.
- My distant relatives will help me getting extra points for permanent residency.
- It is very easy to get permanent residency once I am in Australia.
- My friend or my uncle can help me in making an application for my permanent residency.

Please note that the student visa has its own requirements and it does not lead to direct permanent residency. The student visa is a temporary visa, which ends with your studies. You may wish to apply for a Temporary Graduate visa to find suitable work once you complete your degree program. In this case, the course you select could play an important role but you should not go for a course only because it counts towards the skill requirement. If you have no background for the subject, it is possible that you may not get the Australian study visa in the first place.

International students, after completing their studies in Australia, may wish to explore various migration pathways available to them. There are two main pathways that you may consider after completing your studies in Australia:

## Pathway 1: Temporary Graduate (Subclass 485) visa

Based on which course you have completed in Australia you can move to the relevant graduate visa stream. It is a great option for international students who would like to extend their stay in Australia after completing their studies. It is certainly helpful to those seeking to permanently settle in Australia especially through the General Skilled Migration (GSM) program. It is important to note here that to have access to migration pathways, you must adhere to all the visa conditions prescribed in your student visa. There are two Temporary Graduate visa streams:

a. Graduate Work Stream

b. Post-Study Work Stream

## Some of the Common Criteria for the two visa streams are:

- Have completed a trade certificate, diploma, bachelor degree, graduate diploma, masters or PhD qualification in Australia within the last 6 months.
- Applied for 485 visa within 6 months of completion of your Australian studies.
- Australian studies are registered on CRICOS.
- Must be aged under 50 at time of application.
- Evidence of English Language: If you hold a passport from UK, Ireland, USA, Canada or NZ, you will not need to undertake an English test. Otherwise, you are required to provide evidence of English Language: IELTS, Pearson (PTE Academic), ORT, TOEFL iBT or Cambridge (CAE Advanced).
- Meet all health, character and other visa requirements.
- Once granted, you will have unlimited work rights in Australia for the duration of the visa.

Please note that the above common criteria are only a generic guide and relevant at present. There are additional specific requirements to be met for both the visa streams which are subject to change by the Department of Immigration and Border Protection (DIBP). It is vital to the success of your future application under either of the visa streams, that you seek advice from an experienced Registered Migration Agent.

## Pathway 2: General Skilled Migration (GSM): Permanent or Provisional Residence

The Australian government has implemented the General Skilled Migration Program (GSM) to attract in-demand qualified professionals, including fresh international graduates from Australian universities, for migration to Australia. It is the most popular form of migration to Australia, with 72,840 skilled visas granted in financial year 2015-16 alone. [source: www.border.gov.au].

The GSM program has multiple pathways for applicants to obtain a skilled visa. All visas are based on a Points Test Criteria and the current minimum Points Test Score requirement to be eligible for Skilled Migration is 60 points. The visa options include:

**Skilled Independent visas**—for skilled professionals who do not require sponsorship or nomination by a state/territory government, employer or family member.

**Skilled Nominated visas**—for skilled workers who are nominated by a state/territory government or sponsored by an eligible family member in Australia.

## Medium and Long-term Strategic Skills List (MLTSSL) and STSOL (Short-term Skilled Occupation List) (Previously known as Skilled Occupation Lists)

It is important for international students to note that currently there may be Permanent and Provisional Residency visa options available for graduates in occupations listed on either:

1. Medium and Long-term Strategic Skills List (MLTSSL), or
2. Short-term Skilled Occupation List (STSOL)

Please note that some skill assessment bodies may require post-qualification work experience for an applicant to be eligible to obtain skill assessment in an occupation. The Australian government provides recognition of Australian study to international students who wish to settle in Australia after completing their studies. As a graduate from one of the Australia's CRICOS educational institutes, international students can obtain additional points towards permanent residency visa application under the GSM program, particularly if studying in a regional area in Australia. Students with Australian qualifications also have an advantage as it is easier to obtain a positive assessment for a skilled occupation listed on the Occupation Lists.

## Tips for International students:

- Student visa has its own requirements and it does not lead to permanent residency on its own.
- Your ability to complete the selected course will be judged by both the institution and embassy for the student visa so please do not just take up a course for which you do not have relevant background or in which you don't have the intention to pursue your career.
- You must abide by all the student visa conditions.
- MLTSSL and STSOL professions may change during your studies,

so study a course in which you have deep interest and skill for.

- Keep improving your English as higher level of English Language test score can obtain you additional points in applying for residence visas under Skilled migration.
- Utilize the Temporary Graduate visa after your studies to gain experience in your industry and related area of studies.
- Students can benefit from scoring additional points in the Points Test criteria for their studies in Australia, particularly in a regional area.
- There are conditions around family sponsorship and not all relatives can sponsor you for Skilled migration. Please be clear on who is an "eligible family member".

Please note that in Australia only a Registered Migration Agent with a current MARN number can give migration advice relating to the visa options including permanent residency. It is an excellent opportunity for international students, hence you should only choose a trusted and skilled Registered Migration Agent to assist you with the best possible migration pathway available.

**A few simple steps to improve your chances for getting a permanent residency in Australia include the following:**

1. Complete studies successfully, only then points can be claimed for an Australian Qualification.
2. Keep improving English, as higher level of IELTS score whether PTE Academic, IELTS or another is required for residency.
3. Use after studies work permit to gain experience in the related area of studies.
4. Use an experienced and trusted Registered Migration Agent to work on your residency application.

---

Refer Further Information Section/ Reference for website links from page 225–229.
You are recommended to study the appropriate material beforehand for information assessment.

# 40
# Conclusion

The purpose of the SiA Planner is to enable students to plan, prepare and apply for their education in Australia. It is not a substitute for a professional counselor but rather acts as a bridge between the two. Sometimes, students and also their families become relaxed after assigning their case to an agent thinking it is the agent's job to do all the work on their behalf. While the agent is meant to be your guide, your role is pivotal in the whole process. The SiA Planner has information, direction, structure, and exercises for students who want to actively engage in the process.

The SiA Planner allows students to participate in the application process with adequate knowledge. It also empowers students to communicate their requirements to their counselor and institutions. The awareness and participation of students is critical for their successful study and future in Australia. The SiA planner gives all the required information for the bright future of the students aspiring to study in Australia.

# APPENDIX

# Appendix 1
# Terminologies

### Intake:

Intake is course start date. It is also called commencement date or enrolment date. Australian institutions majorly have two intakes starting in the month of February and July commonly known as Semester One and Semester Two respectively.

### Semester:

Semester is used for term. One term is usually of 6 months. One year may have two kinds of semesters—Semester or Trimester. Trimesters are three semesters per year.

### Offer Letter:

Offer letter is a document issued by the institutions to confirm student eligibility for admission. It is an outcome of student academic and English language capability assessment against the course requirement for which student has applied for admission. Offer letter provides information about course, tuition fees, student personal details, payment requirement to confirm seat, health insurance requirement, refund policy, guardianship information, if needed etc.

Offer letter does not confirm student seat until student makes the payment.

### COE:

Confirmation of Enrolment—COE is the receipt of tuition fees and Health Insurance payment made by student for the confirmation of their seat. COE is required to apply for a visa. If a student has a packaged course, COE is required for each course until highest level including ELICOS if there is any. Visa may get declined if a valid and complete COE is not provided with the visa application.

### Extension Letter:

This is late entry permission requested by student in situations like late visa arrival or non-availability of tickets etc. Some universities are very strict and they do not allow late entry to their courses. Some institutions allow one to two weeks of extension. Ask for extension on time, usually around a week in advance. While asking for extension letter, ensure that deadlines will be met.

## NOOSR:

A guide created by the Australian government to refer to the various categories of Indian universities. It is referred for admission in master's degree by the institutions in Australia. The guide is not available for free access. A student needs to take help of counselor or institution to check the level of their institution.

## GTE:

GTE stands for Genuine & Temporary Entrant—This is the criteria from which both admission and visa applications are judged in Australia as student visa is a temporary visa and it is expected that the intention of applying for admission or student visa is purely studies although students are entitled to various other privileges like work rights etc. Each applicant is assessed under GTE criteria including student dependents.

## Funds Approval:

This is Australian University's checking process to test a student's financial background before asking him to make payment or confirm his seat. A Student must not pay tuition fees until the Fund Approval is received.

## Funds Approval Interview:

Students are interviewed for admission either before the issuance of offer letter or before fund approval.The Student should be ready for the interview at the time of making admission application. Some universities call up on the same day for interview when application is received while others may take a week to interview. Remember an interview call may be received with or without any prior confirmation.

## OSHC (Overseas Health Cover)

OSHC is the student insurance coverage. Insurance is needed for complete duration of the course. It is mandatory to have health cover at the time of applying for visa. If a student is going with family, OSHC of each member is compulsory.

## Medicals:

Each student needs medicals before applying for visa. Medicals refers to all medical tests that a student needs to take and submit the report during his/her visa application.

## TAFE:

TAFE stands for Technical and Further Education. TAFE courses are known as VET courses which is Vocational Education Training. TAFE institutions are government colleges that offer diploma, advance diploma and bachelor degrees. TAFE courses are focused on direct skill creation.

## SSVF:

SSVF is Simplified Student Visa Framework which has replaced the previous Streamline Visa Processing.

# Appendix 2
# List of universities

## 1 Major Groups of Universities in Australia

**Group of Eight universities (Go8)**
The Group of Eight (Go8) comprises Australia's eight leading research universities.

1. The University of Adelaide
2. The Australian National University
3. The University of Melbourne.
4. Monash University
5. The University of New South Wales
6. The University of Queensland
7. The University of Sydney
8. The University of Western Australia

**Australian Technology Network**
The Australian Technology Network of Universities (ATN) brings together five of the most innovative and enterprising universities in Australia.

1. Curtin University of Technology
2. University of South Australia
3. RMIT University
4. University of Technology Sydney
5. Queensland University of Technology

**Sandstone universities of Australia**
Group of Australia's oldest universities.

1. University of Adelaide
2. Australian National University

3. University of Melbourne
4. Monash University
5. University of New South Wales
6. University of Queensland
7. University of Sydney
8. University of Western Australia

## 2 State-wise Universities in Australia

**Australian Capital Territory**

1. Australian National University
2. University of Canberra

**New South Wales**

1. Australian Catholic University
2. Charles Sturt University
3. Macquarie University
4. Southern Cross University
5. University of New England
6. University of New South Wales
7. University of Newcastle
8. University of Sydney
9. University of Technology, Sydney
10. Western Sydney University
11. University of Wollongong

**Northern Territory**

1. Charles Darwin University

**Queensland**

2. Bond University
3. CQ University
4. Griffith University
5. James Cook University

6. Queensland University of Technology
7. University of Queensland
8. University of Southern Queensland
9. University of the Sunshine Coast

**South Australia**

1. Carnegie Mellon University
2. Flinders University
3. Torrens University Australia
4. University College London
5. University of Adelaide
6. University of South Australia

**Tasmania**

1. University of Tasmania

**Victoria**

1. Deakin University
2. Federation University of Australia
3. La Trobe University
4. Monash University
5. RMIT University
6. Swinburne University of Technology University of Divinity
7. University of Melbourne
8. Victoria University

**Western Australia**

1. Curtin University
2. Edith Cowan University
3. Murdoch University
4. University of Notre Dame Australia
5. University of Western Australia

## 3 Ranking summary of the Australian universities

| University | ERA | QS | TIMES | ARWU | US News |
|---|---|---|---|---|---|
| University of Melbourne | 1 | 42 | =33 | 40 | 36= |
| University of Sydney | 2 | 46 | =60 | 82 | 45= |
| Australian National University | 3= | 22 | 47 | 77 | 80= |
| University of Queensland | 3= | 51 | =60 | 55 | 52 |
| University of New South Wales | 4 | 49 | =78 | 101+ | 80= |
| Monash University | 5 | 65 | 74 | 79 | 79 |
| University of Western Australia | 6 | 102 | 125 | 96 | 95= |
| Adelaide University | 7 | 125 | 142 | 101+ | 152= |
| Macquarie University | 8 | 247 | 251+ | 201+ | 267= |
| University of Wollongong | 9 | 218 | 251+ | 301+ | 313= |
| Southern Cross University | 10 | | 501+ | | 896= |
| Tasmania University | 11 | 370 | 301+ | 201+ | 323 |
| Queensland University of Technology | 12 | 276 | 201+ | 201+ | 319= |
| University of Technology, Sydney | 13= | 193 | 251+ | 301+ | 294 |
| Newcastle University | 13= | 245 | 201+ | 301+ | 313= |
| University of South Australia | 14 | 288 | 251+ | | 433= |
| Swinburne University | 15 | 441+ | 351+ | 401+ | 433= |
| Griffith University | 16= | 336 | 251+ | 301+ | 307= |
| Royal Melbourne Institute of Technology | 16= | 252 | 401+ | 401+ | 486= |
| Deakin University | 17 | 355 | 251+ | 201+ | 309= |
| James Cook University | 18 | 340 | 251+ | 201+ | 273 |
| University of Western Sydney | 19 | 551+ | 401+ | 301+ | 384= |
| La Trobe University | 20 | 386 | 351+ | 301+ | 535= |
| Central Queensland University | 21 | 601+ | 401+ | | |
| Charles Darwin University | 22 | 551+ | 251+ | | 803= |
| Murdoch University | 23 | 501+ | 401+ | | 625= |
| Bond University | 24= | 461+ | 501+ | | |
| Southern Cross University | 24= | | 501+ | | |

Contd.

| University | ERA | QS | TIMES | ARWU | US News |
|---|---|---|---|---|---|
| Charles Sturt University | 25 | 701+ | | | 854= |
| Curtin University | 26 | 306 | 401+ | 201+ | 297= |
| University of New England | 27 | 701+ | | | 691= |
| Flinders University | 28 | 551+ | 351+ | 301+ | 471 |
| University of Southern Queensland | 29= | 701+ | 601+ | | |
| Victoria University | 29= | 651+ | 351+ | | 613= |
| Canberra University | 29= | 551+ | 401+ | | |
| Edith Cowan University | 29= | 701+ | 501+ | | 706= |
| Australian Catholic University | 29= | 701+ | 601+ | | |
| Notre Dame University | 29= | | | | |
| Federation University | 29= | | | | |

Source: http://www.australianuniversities.com.au/rankings/#usnewsrankings

ERA: Excellence Research for Australia
QS: QS World University
TIMES: THE Times Higher Education
US News: US News
ARWU: ARWU Shanghai Academic

Refer Further Information Section/ Reference for website links from page 225–229.
You are recommended to study the appropriate material beforehand for information assessment.

# Appendix 3

# Formats of letters for documentation

## 1 ExperienceLetter

### LETTERHEAD

---

DATE:

**To Whomsoever it May Concern**

**First paragraph:**
Mention duration with the definite start and end date, designation along with complete name and employment class if there is any. Specify employment type as FULL TIME/ PART TIME/ CASUAL.

**Second Paragraph:**
Confirm role and responsibility.
Mention any additional accountability handled by the applicant.

**Third Paragraph:**
Bring forth promotions, awards and achievements.

Thanks
Regards
Signature

Full Name
Designation
Contact details
Stamp
**Note:**
**Salary:**
Although it is not necessary to mention salary in the experience letter, it helps if you get the salary mentioned unless you have separate salary slips available with Form 16 or ITRs. If you are paid in cash, it must coincide with your job category. A cash salary payment invites scrutiny as it is not a preferred option of the assessment for the officers. You need to provide details about the reasons for being paid in cash and explain it well in your application.

# 2 Letter of Recommendation (LOR)

## LETTERHEAD

---

DATE:

**To Whomsoever it May Concern**

**First paragraph:**
Use this part to establish the relationship between the referee and the student. Here the referee also establishes his/her credibility by stating his role and responsibility within the organization.

**Second Paragraph:**
Highlight skills, talent, performance and achievements of the applicant. The referee should give specific examples pertinent to the student. Add more paragraphs if needed but stick to the specific information.

**Closing Paragraph:**
This paragraph should contain the overall opinion and recommendation of the student.

Thanks
Regards
Signature

Full Name
Designation
Contact details
Stamp

# 3 Education Loan Sanction Letter

**To be printed on bank letterhead; stamped and signed by the approving authority.**

The bank Education Loan Letter must have following information:

1. Date:
2. Name of applicant (student):
3. Parents/Spouse Details:
4. Name and Address of Bank:
5. Name of the course:
6. University/ College Name:
7. Loan Amount sanctioned:
8. Loan Category (Education Loan/ Personal/ Term):
9. Validity period of Loan:
10. Interest Rate per month:
11. Repayment period and plan:
12. Guarantor's name:
13. Co-borrower's name:
14. Security/Collateral (what has been mortgaged?):
15. Disbursement details:
16. Branch manager signature
17. Bank stamp/ Seal
18. Business card of the bank manager

**NOTE:**

- Contact details of the bank must be clearly mentioned on bank letterhead.
- Keep a bank attested copy of the documents that you have mortgaged.
- You can add more information if that is necessary for your application.

# 4 Education Loan Disbursement Letter

**(Needed on bank letterhead with phone numbers)**

**LETTERHEAD**

---

DATE:

**To Whomsoever it May Concern**

This is to confirm that we have released the first instalment of the loan sanctioned to Mr............................ in the form of a Draft No/ Telegraphic transfer No....................... for AUD........................... dated ........................... in the favor of.................... (University/ College name).

This draft has been issued towards the tuition fees and overseas health cover of Mr/Ms ............................ and was disbursed out of the Education Loan sanctioned.

________________________

(Bank Manager)

STAMP
DATED:

**NOTE:**

- If you have paid your first instalment of the tuition fee through the education loan, disbursement letter will be needed at the time of your visa application submission.
- If you have paid your health insurance or accommodation booking fee through the education loan, please add complete details in the letter.

# 5 Affidavit of Support

**(On stamp paper (INR 20/-)**
**(PARENTS)**

We Mr......................... and Mrs/Ms.................... parents of.................... Resident of ..................................do hereby solemnly affirm and declare as under:

That our son/daughter has received admission in (course) ......................................... at ........................................................... (university/College name), in Australia starting on...........................................................................(course start date).

That we have gone through the contents of the course and we are satisfied about the recognition of the institute and program both.

That we are aware the total fees to study the course is AUD................... and total living expenses for the whole course duration is AUD..............................................

That we have made all financial arrangements towards the tuition and living expenses required by our child during his studies. We have ..............family members. Both/One of us has well earning job/ business and our annual income is ............................

That we have INR............................. available towards (student name) .......................... education in Australia and we have enough income and savings to support the regular needs of the all the family members staying in India.

That we will financially support our son/daughter for his/her education in Australia for the period of studies.

PLACE: .......................................
DATE: .......................................
DEPONENT1 .......................................
DEPONENT2 .......................................

# 6 Affidavit of Support

**(On stamp paper (INR 20/-)**
**(Relative/ Friends)**

We/I Mr.................. or/ and Mrs/Ms........................... (specify relationship) of........................., Resident of .....................do hereby solemnly affirm and declare as under:

That (student name) ..................... has received admission in (course) ........................................... at ........................ (university/College name), in Australia starting on..........................................course start date).

That I/we have gone through the contents of the course and I/we am/are satisfied about the recognition of the institute and program both.

That I/we am/are aware of the total tuition fees to study the course is AUD............ and total living expenses for the whole course duration is AUD..........................

I/we have ..............family members and ............... dependents. Both/One of us has well earning job/ business and my/our annual income is ...........................

That I/we have INR.............................. available towards (student name) .......................... education in Australia and I/we have enough income and savings to support the regular needs of the all the family members staying in India.

That I/we will financially support (student name) for his/her education in Australia for the period of studies.

PLACE: ........................................
DATE: ........................................
DEPONENT1 ........................................
DEPONENT2 ........................................

**NOTE:**
You should personalize the affidavit of support with more information. Affidavit needs to clarify:

- Why the person is sponsoring the student?
- When and how they want student to return their money, if they need to?
- If the money given is loan or gift. If it is a gift, why giving such huge amount of gift?

- How much of the amount declared will be used to sponsor the student?
- What are the sponsors' personal financial liabilities?
- Information about sponsor's profession and family responsibilities, including children and dependent family members, including non-working spouse and parents.
- What are the savings and property investments of the sponsor which convey that sponsor can afford to give extra money to student for his/ her studies and still can easily look after his/her own personal responsibilities of the family?

| 7 Funds Details | | | | | |
|---|---|---|---|---|---|
| Once funds are collected, you should bring all the details together in one or two pages with important information required for the visa file processing. Personalise this information for your file. | | | | | |
| Student Full Name | | | | | |
| Tuition Fees per year | | | Course | | |
| Living expenses for Self/ family | | | University | | |
| OSHC for complete course duration | | | Course Start Date | | |
| **Airfare** | | | | | |
| Sponsor Full Name | Relationship with Student | Funds Category | Balance available | Source of Major Deposit | Supporting Document Available |
| ABCDEF | Father | Saving Account | | Salary Account | Monthly salary transaction details |
| GHIKL | Mother | Fixed Deposit | | Rental income | Rent agreement and rental receipt |
| MNOPQ PVT. LTD. | Father's Business | Current Account | | Business | Bank statement |
| Bank name | Self | Education Loan | | Property/ Fixed Deposit mortgaged | Approved Education Loan Letter |
| | Self | Advance payment towards tuition fees | | Personal saving/ education loan | COE from university |
| ABCD | Uncle/ Aunty | Saving Account | | salary/ business | Bank statement |
| Total Funds Available for student expenses | | | | | |

Contd.

| Sponsor income details and relationship proof | | | | | |
|---|---|---|---|---|---|
| **Sponsor Name** | **Relationship with student** | **Occupation** | **Income Per year** | **If ITRs of 3 years available** | **Relationship Document proof** |
| | | | | | |
| | | | | | |
| | | | | | |
| | | | | | |

| Sponsors Liability, Savings, Property Investment Details | | | | | |
|---|---|---|---|---|---|
| **Sponsor Name** | **Relationship with student** | **Total family members** | **Number of dependents (non-earning members)** | **Properties and savings for own family members** | **Amount giving to student for studies** |
| | | | | | |
| | | | | | |
| | | | | | |
| | | | | | |

# 8 Application for Conditional Offer Letter

To

The Admission Officer,
International Office,
University of ....................................................................................................
Sydney, Australia.

**Subject:** Request for conditional letter of offer

Provisional degree awaited

**Personal Details:** FULL NAME
Date of Birth
Passport Number

Dear Officer,
I ...............................................................,am applying for admission in Masters of Business Administration at University of ...........................................................
I would like to inform you that my provisional degree certificate is awaited. I have completed the bachelor's degree and all the mark sheets are attached with the application. I have also attached my certificate.
I request you to kindly process my application for conditional letter of offer such that I can start working on the financial arrangement of my studies.
The provisional degree completion certificate/ full degree will be available within 3 weeks and I will submit it as soon as it is received.

Thanks & Regards

NAME

Contact Details

# 9 Application for IELTS Exemption

To

The Admission Officer,
International Office,
University of ..............................................................................................
Sydney, Australia.

**Subject:** Request for IELTS Exemption

**Personal Details:** FULL NAME
Date of Birth
Passport Number

Dear Officer,
I ..........................................................,am applying for admission in Masters of Business Administration at University of ..................................................
I would like to inform you that I have excellent communication skills. This is proven through my academic performances which have been conducted in English throughout my studies.
I have completed my studies from ................................ school where both the studies and the exams are conducted in English medium. I have scored A+ in English subject in class X and 80% in English subject in class XII. I have participated in debates and performances conducted in English. I completed my bachelor's degree in English medium as well and I am working in a multinational corporation where English is the only mode of communication.
I am confident that I will be able to study well in Australia with my current English language level. I have the required level of English and I request you to exempt me from taking an English test. I understand that if I am given an English exemption, I may get interviewed by the admission or the visa officer to check my English skills in person. I also understand that if my faculty thinks it is important for me to take the test before admission, I am ready to take up the test.
Since I am working, it helps me to save time if I get the exemption. I look forward to your consideration.

Thanks & Regards
NAME

Contact Details

**Note:**

- Students are not advised to apply for exemption unless their performance in English is exceptional.
- You may get interviewed by the officers to check your English level.
- Visa officer may not accept the exemption and ask you to provide an English score at the time of visa approval.

# 10 Application for Credit Transfer

To

The Admission Officer,
International Office,
University of ........................................................................................
Sydney, Australia.

**Subject:** Request for credit transfer

**Personal Details:** FULL NAME........................................................
Date of Birth........................................................
Passport Number..............................................

Dear Officer,

I .........................................................,am applying for admission in Bachelor of Business Administration at University of ......................................................
I would like to inform you that I have studied Advance Diploma of Commerce from ......................................................college recognized by ........................
........................................... I have compared my subjects with the course content of the Bachelor of Business degree and I find that I have successfully completed 15 units in India.
I request you to kindly assess my application for credit exemption towards the subjects that I have already studied in India.
I understand that credit transfer is a complex process and it is also influenced by the grades scored by me in each subject. I have attached the complete syllabus of my course studied in India.
I request you to kindly process my admission application with credit assessment.

Thanks & Regards

NAME

Contact Details

**Note:**

- You must attach complete syllabus of the course with application for credit assessment.
- You must compare subjects well before making an application.
- Your application will go to the faculty for assessment. Hence, credit assessment applications have longer processing time.

# 11 Application for Late Entry Permission

To

The Admission Officer,
International Office,
University of ......................
Sydney, Australia.

**Subject:** Approval needed for late enrolment

**Personal Details:** FULL NAME.............................................
Date of Birth................................................
Student ID Number......................................

Dear Officer,

I ........................, have secured admission in .................................. course and my visa application decision is pending at the Australian High Commission. I need to provide an extension letter to the embassy for the further processing of my application.

I request you to kindly provide me approval to enrol after one week of the course start date.

I have made my travel arrangements and I am ready to fly as soon as my visa confirmation is received.

I understand that I am responsible for catching up the missed classes.

Thanks & Regards

NAME

Contact Details

**Note:**

- Be aware that not all the institutions provide late entry permission.
- Late arrivals are not accepted in some courses.
- You must have written confirmation from the university for late enrollment. If you delay your campus arrival after receiving visa and without informing the university, you may not be accepted in the class.

# 12 Application for Enrolment Deferment

To

The Admission Officer,
International Office,
University of ......................
Sydney, Australia.

**Subject:** Enrolment deferment needed

**Personal Details:** FULL NAME...............................................
Date of Birth.................................................
Student ID Number.........................................

Dear Officer,

I ........................................................................, have secured admission in ........................................................ Course. Due to the delay in the visa processing, I have missed the latest enrolment date at the university.

My visa application is still active at the embassy and I need to provide deferred enrolment confirmation evidence for the further processing of my visa application for the next intake starting on ........................................................................

I request you to kindly provide me new confirmation and enrolment.

Thanks & Regards

NAME

Contact Details

**Note:**

- You must provide new confirmation of enrolment if you miss the enrolment date and also the extension date.
- If you do not provide confirmation, you visa application may get closed.

# Appendix 4
# Sample letters

## 1 Letter of Recommendation (LOR) from work

**LETTERHEAD OF THE ORGANISATION**

---

**DATE:**

**To Whomsoever it May Concern**

Mr ABCD has worked as an intern at CDEF for seven months (from ........................................ to ..........................................). I take the pleasure of recommending him for the Master's program at your university.

During his time at CDEF, Mr ABCD has assisted the senior structural engineer in various aspects. His first challenging project was the structural design of a beautiful(NAME) hotel in Jammu, where he processed and analyzed the steel beam and columns. I was impressed by his ability to perform each task quickly and efficiently. He has excellent interpersonal skills and he has worked effectively with the other team members.

Apart from this, his empathetic ability is amazing. I realized that when he was successfully trained to work on STAAD.PRO V8i, used for modelling and analysis of the structures; he went on to work fluently on several other cutting-edge projects such as design of industrial and commercial structures. ABCD has outstanding organizational skills. He was successfully able to complete multiple tasks with favorable results.

I strongly recommend Mr ABCD for the admission to master's degree in structural engineering at your university. During his short period of involvement with us, he has been a great asset to our organization.

Please feel free to contact me should you require any further information.

Signature

Full Name
Designation
Contact details

# 2 Letter of Recommendation (LOR) for education

**LETTERHEAD OF THE COLLEGE**

Reference Number (if it is followed by the college) Date: 14/2/2017

Recommendation Letter

I would like to recommend my student Mr ABCD to your university's graduate admission committee as an applicant to the master's program in Structural Engineering. He was my student for three years. I was his instructor for the course on EARTHQUAKE RESISTANT DESIGN OF STRUCTURES and assisted him in various lab work. He always showed keenness to study further and it is very clear to me that he has the requisites for a master's degree.

I have had a chance to observe not only his academics but also his leadership qualities during the group activities. He actively took part in the seminars and has got sound communication skills. I remember him giving a presentation at the seminar on architecture and concept of Burj Khalifa, Dubai. He successfully completed his final year group project under my guidance on "SEISMIC DESIGN OF ELEVATED WATER TANK". During the group project meeting I came to know about his intellectual capacity and research oriented approach.

ABCD has maintained a good balance of activities throughout his engineering studies. I enthusiastically recommend him for post graduate studies at your prestigious university. I wish him all the best for his higher studies.

Signature

Full Name<br>
Designation<br>
Department and contact details

**Note:**

- Mention specific details on what and where student performance was observed.

# 3 Successful Statement of Purpose (SOP)

I started my internship at ABCD Associates, Structural consultant in Noida, earlier this year. After seven months of internship (March 2014-September 2014), I want to undertake graduate studies in Master of Engineering (Honors) at University of Sydney, Australia.

After concluding my studies as an undergraduate from ABCD, UPTU, with first division, doing a specialization in a specific field of Civil Engineering has always been on my mind. So, I took up this internship at a designing firm as it is important to have a closer look at your field before commencing higher studies. I assisted the Senior Structural Engineer in several challenging projects such as designing industrial complexes and commercial buildings where I learned to work on the softwares like Staad. ProV8i, Etab is used for modeling and analysing the structure.

Initially, my father, an Architect, encouraged me to go for Civil Engineering. After completing my second year in B.Tech, I signed up for one-month industrial training at a residential apartment site. It was here that I was first exposed to the world of Civil Engineering. After that my hunger to explore this field has been increasing. Mr ABCD, Managing Partner at the designing firm, who was also my mentor there encouraged my ambition and told me that I have the potential to pursue higher studies. Mr ABC, an Alumni of University of Sheffield UK, completed his Master's Degree in Structural Engineering.

While going through my graduation mark-sheets you will notice that I have conceded nine backlogs during my initial years of B.Tech, maximum being in third semester. I would just like to stress on the point, that I may have started with backlogs but that didn't make me grow despondent. Instead I worked hard for the rest of my graduation and completed it without any backlogs in the final year. I consider this as an improvement on my part. Also, I never had any backlogs in any of the core subjects i.e. Structure Analysis, RCC and Earthquake Design. I'd like to assure you these backlogs will not be any hindrance for my postgraduation and there will be no unwelcome results during the course study.

In selecting the University of Sydney, I went through the Course structure of the program and was influenced by the subjects that are taught in Major. I am particularly excited to study Structural Dynamics and Earthquake Engineering as this subject is close to my final year project in B.Tech. I have also been in contact with many alumina & seniors and they have told me about the multicultural and friendly environment in Australia. I believe that under the guidance of experienced professors and industry professionals, this graduation course will shape my future and will give me the opportunity to excel in the field of Civil Engineering.

Thanks
**ABCD**

**Result: Successful visa (Direct Visa Approval)**

**What is good about the SOP:**

**Focus:** Student focus and reason for selecting the course is very clear.

**Ability:** He has proved his academic capability to study the course in spite of backlogs.

**Responsibility:** Student comes across as responsible; he has tried to gain knowledge and discuss with important people before deciding to study in Australia. He has conveyed the specifics appropriately.

# 4 Unsuccessful Statement of Purpose (SOP)

I ABCD completed my Matriculation in 2012 with 73% from XYZ school & Senior Secondary from XYZ in 2014 scoring 66%. I appeared for IELTS on ABCDEFG and scored 5.5 overall. I want to pursue my Diploma leading to Bachelor of Business Administration from ABCDEF institute, Melbourne. I have chosen this course as I have interest in the managerial side of business and I want to learn more about it. This course will help me to gain managerial level training for clerical & administrative work. The course will prepare me to explore more specialized areas such as accounting, marketing, finance, International business and human resources.

I have chosen ABCDEF institute as it provides students with the practical knowledge which helps them to learn through their own experiences. Most important, the fees are quite affordable for me. Also, the college offers a wide range of scholarships to assist students from many different backgrounds. This helps the students to pay their tuition fees. Its courses are professionally managed & the staff is highly qualified.

I selected Australia because Australia provides quality education & education obtained from Australian universities is recognized all over the world. India also has good institutes but competition for getting into those institutes is very tough. Also, I will get global exposure by studying this course from Australia.

After completion of this course, I would be coming back to India & can work in various fields like marketing, finance sector, operations, accounting & can work as strategic consultant, manager etc. I can earn approx.30,000 to 45,000/-per month.

Thanks
ABCD

**Result: Unsuccessful visa (Direct visa rejection)**

**What is not addressed properly:**

1. **Career Progression:** Student has just passed class XII and he wants to start his career from a managerial position. It shows lack of awareness towards the actual outcome of the course and progression pathway.
2. **Random data without any relevance:** He has mentioned about scholarships. However, it is not clear if student has received any scholarship or he will be applying for it.
3. **Varied Career Options:** The career outcome is extremely confusing. Student says he can work in marketing, finance, operations, accounting & can also work as strategic consultant or manager.

**Areas of improvement:**

Being an undergraduate student, he needs to bring out his career progress pathway. Student is expected to give clear career path be it accounts, marketing or HR. Statements must be clear.

# 5 Successful Visa after interview (SOP)

I am ABCD and I live in Mumbai with my family. I am very happy at getting this opportunity to submit my statement of purpose with regard to my intention to study Masters of Professional Accounting in XYZ, Melbourne campus, Australia. Today, the world is developing at a very fast pace; generalized and bookish knowledge in any field is not sufficient. I have to break the mould, come out of the box and do things differently. I aspire for a career which would allow me to pursue my love for Accounting.

I am a hardworking and sincere student. I have passed 12th standard with 79% from Maharashtra Higher Secondary Education Board in Mumbai. After that I completed Bachelor of Commerce from Mumbai University in the year 2014 with second class. I completed Master of Commerce from IGNOU in the year 2016. Value of a foreign degree is very high to get position in a well-known company. So, I decided to complete my further education from well-known foreign university.

In order to get admission in a foreign university, IELTS or PTE exams are mandatory. So I started preparation for IELTS and I have given IELTS. I got overall 5.5 band. As my IELTS score is low compared to the entry requirement, so I will be doing 10 weeks ELICOS course before my main course so that my English Language is enhanced & my English is of the same level as of the other students in my class.

After I decided to study abroad, I did research for my further study and I found many courses but I want to make my future in accounting field as I have keen interest and I have been studying Accounting from 11th standard and I am good in Accounting. The course which I want to study, Master of Professional Accounting is relevant to my previous study. The duration of the course is 2 year full time at Melbourne campus. The course aims to provide local and international graduates with the necessary knowledge in accounting and the role accounting plays in providing information to support business activities. In addition to providing a professionally recognized qualification, the course comprises a mix of accounting, finance, legal and economics subjects which collectively provide a range of essential business skills and knowledge that are necessary for employment in today's dynamic business environment. The core subjects are Accounting Systems & Processes, Management Accounting for Costs & Control, Financial Accounting, Decision Support Tools, Auditing, Economics for Business, and Current Developments in Accounting Thought. Elective subjects are Human Resource Management, Values and Conflicts in Organizations, Management Theory & Practice, and International Business.The Master of Professional Accounting will provide me with training in the technical aspects of the preparation of accounting data, develop my skills in the application of accounting information to solving problems and making decisions;

and develop my knowledge and skills in related professional disciplines such as finance, taxation, auditing and management. I am sure that with my academic standards and strong motivation, keenness, positive attitude and with the aid of this program, I will be able to make a significant contribution to my future career at an accelerated pace.

It is an uphill task to find a quality institute and get admission into it in India. In addition to that, the course structure does not give much scope of practical learning. Also, I did consider education options at UK, USA, Canada etc. but the lifestyle, affordable tuition fees and recognition of education worldwide made me choose Australia as my destination for further education. Moreover, Australia is an international leader in the field of accountancy and has a reputation for excellence in this sector. Institutions in Australia offer World Class Infrastructure and Teaching Facilities and therefore offer better learning environment as compared to Indian Institutions. By choosing to study in Australia, one gets a chance to join thousands of students from Australia and all over the world, who are discovering new friends and opportunities in this beautiful country.

Considering all these things, I decided to study in Australia because the value of and Australian Degree is the best recommendation for not only India but also for Asian Countries for fruitful future and better prospects. Australia is known as 3rd best place to study and live after USA and Canada. Australia is giving an option of post study work which is an opportunity for International students to work even after studies and gain international experience. Now a days Australia is one of the emerging countries offering variety of courses of different specializations, which are very well recognized at international level and especially in India. Australia, apart from being a prominent learning centre, offers a congenial environment for advanced studies. In addition to this, Australian culture being so adaptable, open, and welcoming will provide me a strong platform to enhance my cross culture knowledge. I will return back to my home country enriched with academic and personal growth, and equipped with an Australian degree my future prospects will be brighter and will provide me an opportunity to demonstrate my specialized knowledge, skills and techniques to win a rewarding and successful career in field of accounting.

Master of professional Accounting course is offered at University of Queensland, Griffith University, and James cook University. When I compared all these Universities, I found that curriculum and fee structure offered at XYZ was meeting my requirements. XYZ of Australia provides high quality education in all streams to international students in a congenial and supportive learning environment. XYZ is a very famous university and I got good reviews about it from the internet and my friends. XYZ treats every student with respect and dignity. This university has qualified staff on hand to help students make the best course decisions to attain their academic goals. Master of Professional Accounting in Australia provides me an opportunity to extend my knowledge and skills in accounting field. The program will boost my career advancement prospects and provide a competitive advantage. XYZ is one of Australia's top ranked universities for "success in getting a job", with a 5-star rating in the 2014 Good Universities Guide. So I am confident of the value of an XYZ degree in the job market. Moreover, it is a university offering career oriented degrees.

After the completion of my Master's at XYZ, I will acquire practical Accounting skills and also have a sound background in business. I will seek a job which will utilize my Accounting, business and management skills.

After getting the Australian degree I will return back to India. Because there are many Indian companies providing accounting, taxation and other financial services to Australian and other overseas clients, I can get good opportunities in India. I can get opportunities as Auditor, Financial Manager, Financial Banker and my salary would be 5 to 6 lakh per annum.

I am aware of obligations of a student visa i.e. I must get enrolment in a registered course and maintain 80% attendance and 50% score in academics. I must maintain health insurance (OSHC) during the time I am in Australia. I must keep the education institution and DIBP informed of my current address in Australia. I have to notify them of any changes within 7days. I cannot work more than 40 hours per fortnight when course is in session and I cannot change my course provider for the first six months.

Kindly consider my statement of purpose to study in Australia so that I could make my career in Accounting and have an excellent future by pursuing the Master of Professional Accounting.

Thanking you,
**ABCD**

**Result: Successful visa after interview**

**Areas of improvement:**

Student has covered most of the important areas and he has repeated the information although he has also given some specific information as well. By reading the SOP, reader can make out that the student has made efforts to understand the requirement of further studies in Australia. However, an interview call may help the visa officer to understand if the student is clear about his statements given in the SOP.

# 6 Visa Refusal Letter

**Purpose of sharing a rejection letter.**
Reading a rejection letter will help you understand the expectations of the visa officer. This will assist you to review your application and address your situation appropriately.

(Only appropriate material has been taken)

Dear **********************

**Notification of refusal of application for a Student (Temporary) (class TU) Student (subclass 500) visa**

**Refused Applicant**

I wish to advise you that the application for this visa has been refused on ******************* for the following applicant:

**Client Name** **********************
**Date of Birth** **********************

The applicant did not satisfy the provisions of the Migration Regulations 1994.
The attached Decision Record provides detailed information about this decision as it applies to this applicant.

**Review rights**

There is no right of merits review for this decision.

**Receiving this Letter**

As this letter was sent to you by email, you are taken to have received it at the end of the day it was transmitted.

**Questions about this decision**

The Department cannot consider your visa application any further.

## DECISION RECORD

**Application details**

Visa Class Student (Temporary) (class TU) Student (subclass 500)

Stream (main applicant only) Higher Education Sector

Date of visa application *********************

Transaction reference number ********************

Application ********************

File number ********************

Visa Application ********************

Client Name ********************

Date of Birth ********************

Client ID 44281438080

Visa Subclass Stream Higher Education Sector

The applicant's claims

The applicant applied for a Student (Temporary) (class TU) Student (subclass 500) visa.

## Information and evidence considered

I am a delegated decision maker under section 65 of the Migration Act 1958. In reaching my decision, I have considered the following:

- Relevant legislation contained in the Migration Act and Migration Regulations 1994
- Information contained in the Department's Procedures Advice Manual 3
- Documents and information provided by the applicant(s)

## Findings

On the basis of all the information available to me, including the documents and information the applicant provided, I find that the criteria for the grant of a Student visa are not met by the applicant.

## Reasons

I have assessed the application and the reasons for my decision are detailed below.

An application for a Student visa has been made by the applicant. A visa cannot be granted unless the relevant criteria specified in the Migration Act and the Migration Regulations are satisfied.

In this case, I am not satisfied that clause 500.212 in Schedule 2 of the Migration Regulations is satisfied. This clause provides that:

## 500.212

The applicant is a genuine applicant for entry and stay as a student because:

(a) the applicant intends genuinely to stay in Australia temporarily, having regard to:

(i) the applicant's circumstances; and

(ii) the applicant's immigration history; and

(iii) if the applicant is a minor—the intentions of a parent, legal guardian or spouse of the applicant; and

(iv) any other relevant matter; and

(b) the applicant intends to comply with any conditions subject to which the visa is granted, having

## regard to:

(i) the applicant's record of compliance with any condition of a visa previously held by the applicant (if any); and

(ii) the applicant's stated intention to comply with any conditions to which the visa may be subject; and

(iii) any other relevant matter.

This clause is also known as the genuine temporary entrant criterion.
Ministerial Direction No 69—Assessing the genuine temporary entrant criterion for Student and Student Guardian visa applications sets out the factors that must be taken into account when assessing the genuine temporary entrant criterion for Student visa applications. This Ministerial Direction is made in accordance with section 499 of the Migration Act. Further information is available at: www.border.gov.au/StudyinginAustralia/Documents/directionno—69.pdf

**In summary, these factors include:**

- the applicant's circumstances in their home country, including the applicant's economic situation, political and civil unrest in the applicant's home country, the extent of the applicant's personal ties to their home country, whether the applicant has sound reasons for not studying in their home country if a similar course is available, and military service commitments that would present a significant incentive for the applicant not to return to their home country

- the applicant's potential circumstances in Australia, including the extent of the applicant's ties with Australia that present a strong incentive to remain in Australia, evidence that the student visa program may be used to circumvent the intention of the migration program; whether the Student visa or the Student Guardian is being used to maintain ongoing residence; the applicant's knowledge of living in Australia, and whether the primary and secondary applicants have entered into a relationship of concern

- the value of the course to the applicant's future, including the course's consistency with the applicant's current education level, whether the course will assist the applicant to gain employment in their home country, relevance of the course to the applicant's past or future employment in their home country or a third country, and remuneration and career prospects in the applicant's home country or a third country to be gained from the course

- the applicant's immigration history, including visa and travel history for Australia and other countries, previous visa applications for Australia or other countries, and previous travels to Australia or other countries
- if the applicant is a minor, the intentions of a parent, legal guardian or spouse of the applicant

Any other matter relevant to the applicant's intention to stay in Australia temporarily must also be considered. These factors have been weighed up to make an overall decision. In considering whether the applicant met the genuine temporary entry criterion I had regard to the following factors, consistent with clause 500.212 and Ministerial Direction No 69. The factors were used to weigh up the applicant's circumstances as a whole, in reaching a finding about whether they satisfy the genuine temporary entrant criterion.
I have taken into consideration the documents provided in your application along with the information that you provided in a telephone interview with the Departmental Officer at the Australian High Commission New Delhi on ******************.

I have considered your circumstances in your home country. You completed a ***********************in ***********************and have not studied or worked since that time, aside from helping your father in his business. In your application you have not clearly demonstrated the benefit that undertaking the proposed courses in Australia would provide to your career prospects. I therefore have concerns as to your desire now to undertake further studies in Australia. I therefore am not satisfied you have been able to demonstrate ties that would serve as a significant incentive to return to your home country.
I have also considered your potential circumstances in Australia. You are proposing to undertake English and a ***********************in Australia. On *********************** a Departmental Officer from the Australian High Commission New Delhi investigated your intention to stay in Australia temporarily. The Departmental Officer interviewed you via telephone and the following concerns were highlighted: you did not clearly demonstrate that you had conducted research into your proposed study; you displayed limited knowledge of the content and structure of the proposed course. It is expected that a student who is outlaying a significant amount of money to undertake a course, would have the ability to provide knowledge about the education provider and their proposed studies. I am not satisfied that you have a realistic knowledge of your provider and your proposed studies. I am therefore not satisfied that you have illustrated a genuine intention to undertake the proposed study in Australia.

I have considered the value of this course to your future. I find that in your application you have not clearly demonstrated the benefit that undertaking the proposed courses in Australia would provide to your career prospects. You have stated that upon your return to India you intend to work in your father's business with plans of expansion. Although you have provided a study plan you have not clearly shown how you will achieve this and how an overseas qualification will assist you in attaining this goal. Throughout the interview conducted you also demonstrated limited knowledge about how the course would benefit your future career prospects upon returning to India upon completion of the proposed course. Therefore, I am not satisfied that you have demonstrated the value of your proposed course to your future.

I have taken into consideration your previous immigration history. As you had no immigration history to consider that may be beneficial or adverse to your application, this aspect was not relevant to my assessment.

As you are over 18 years of age, the intentions of your parent, legal guardian or spouse was not relevant to my assessment.

I have considered whether there is any other relevant matter. However, in this case I have determined that there are no other relevant matters.

I have considered all of the information provided by you in support of your application. On balance, I am not satisfied that the information you have provided regarding your circumstances in your home country, potential circumstances in Australia and the value of your proposed course to your future are sufficient to demonstrate that you are a genuine temporary entrant.

## Conclusion

After weighing up these factors as a whole, I am not satisfied that the applicant intends genuinely to stay temporarily in Australia.

## Decision

As clause 500.212 is not met by the applicant, I find the criteria for the grant of Student visa are not met by the applicant. Therefore, I refuse the application by the applicant for Student visa.

## Assessment against the criteria of other subclasses in class TU

As the application was not made on Form 157G (Application for a Student Guardian visa), I have not considered the application against the subclass 590 Student Guardian visa criteria in this visa class.

Yours sincerely

**********************

# Bibliography Source

Australian government – DIBP | Year – N.D. | Student visa (subclass 500) | cited on 19/1/2017 from https://www.border.gov.au/Trav/Visa-1/500-

Australian government – DIBP | Year – N.D. | Student visa financial capacity requirements | cited on 19/1/2017 from https://www.border.gov.au/Trav/Stud/More/Student-Visa-Living-Costs-and-Evidence-of-Funds

Australian High Commission, New Delhi, India, Bhutan | Acceptable financial institutions for funds and loans – Visas and Migration | cited on 19/1/2017 from http://india.embassy.gov.au/ndli/vm_studyloans.html

Australian government – DIBP | Year – N.D. | Genuine temporary entrant | cited on 19/1/2017 from https://www.border.gov.au/Trav/Stud/More/Genuine-Temporary-Entrant

Australian government – DIBP | Year – N.D. | Genuine temporary entrant | cited on 19/1/2017 from https://www.border.gov.au/StudyinginAustralia/Documents/direction-no-69.pdf

Nib | Year N.D. | Overseas students | cited on 19/1/2017 from https://www.nib.com.au/overseas-students

Australian High Commission, New Delhi, India, Bhutan | Representatives of Australian education institutions in India | cited on 19/1/2017 from http://india.embassy.gov.au/ndli/study3.html

# Acronyms & Abbreviations

AQF: Australian Qualification Framework

COE: Confirmation of Enrollment

EAP: English for Academic Purposes

ELICOS: English Language Intensive Course for Overseas Students

ICT: Information and Communication Technology

IPRS: International Postgraduate Research Scholarships

IDP: International Development Program

IELTS: International English Language Testing System

IPRS: International Postgraduate Research Scholarships

LOR: Letters of Reference/ Letters of Recommendation

MPA: Masters of Professional Accounting

OSHC: Overseas Health Insurance Cover

PG: Post Graduate

PhD: Doctor of Philosophy

ROI: Return on Investment

SiA: Study in Australia

SOP: Statement of Purpose

SSSVF: Simplified Student Visa Framework

UG: Under Graduate

# Further Information Section

## Section 1

### 1 Why Study in Australia?

https://www.studyinaustralia.gov.au
https://www.timeshighereducation.com/features/worlds-most-international-universities-2017
http://www.universitas21.com/news/details/61/u21-rankings-of-national-higher-education-systems-2012
http://www.universityrankings.com.au/qs-australian-rankings.html
https://www.studyinaustralia.gov.au/global/australian-education/education-system/esos-act

### 2 Where to Study in Australia?

http://www.australianuniversities.com.au/rankings/
http://www.universityrankings.com.au/qs-australian-rankings.html
http://www.shanghairanking.com/World-University-Rankings-2016/Australia.html
https://www.timeshighereducation.com/world-university-rankings/2017/world-ranking#!/page/0/length/25/locations/AU/sort_by/rank/sort_order/asc/cols/stats
https://www.atn.edu.au/
https://go8.edu.au/
http://www.teqsa.gov.au/for-students
http://cricos.education.gov.au/default.aspx
https://www.tafecourses.com.au/?gclid=CjwKEAiA79zDBRCgyf2FgeiY-CESJABzr0BMCZI_AsRoBJVVVJ5kSmJXZCovkjpaLLahSZvKci6iLhoCNrrw_wcB
http://www.studyinaustralia.gov.au/global/australian-education/universities-and-higher-education/list-of-australian-universities
http://www.teqsa.gov.au/national-register/search/provider
http://cricos.education.gov.au/Institution/InstitutionSearch.aspx

**Dedicated websites for the education provided in the different states.**

http://www.study.vic.gov.au/en/Pages/default.aspx
http://www.studymelbourne.vic.gov.au/
http://www.industry.nsw.gov.au/invest-in-nsw/industry-opportunities/education/studynsw
http://www.studycbr.com.au/

http://www.studyperth.com.au/
http://www.studytasmania.tas.gov.au/
http://www.studynt.nt.gov.au/

## 3 What to Study in Australia?

https://www.studyinaustralia.gov.au/global/australian-education/education-system
http://www.teqsa.gov.au/for-students
http://www.aqf.edu.au/aqf/in-detail/aqf-levels/
http://www.navitasenglish.edu.au/courses/academic-pathways/direct-entry-agreements/
https://corporate.studygroup.com/higher-education/australia
http://www.kaplan.edu.au/pathways/

## 5 Cost of Education in Australia

https://www.studyinaustralia.gov.au/global/live-in-australia/living-costs
http://www.border.gov.au/Trav/Visa/Fees
https://internationaleducation.gov.au/endeavour%20program/scholarships-and-fellowships/about/pages/default.aspx
https://www.studyinaustralia.gov.au/SIASearch/SIAScholarshipsList.aspx?ModuleId=13&Keyword
http://www.australia.gov.au/information-and-services/education-and-training/scholarships

## 6 Profile Evaluation

http://cricos.education.gov.au/
http://www.border.gov.au/Trav/Visa-1/500-

## 7 Decision to Study in Australia

http://india.embassy.gov.au/ndli/study3.html
http://www.aaeri.in/members.html

# Section 2

## 10 English Profile

https://www.ielts.org/what-is-ielts/ielts-for-migration/australia
https://www.mq.edu.au/study/other-study-options/english-language-courses/english-language-courses
http://pearsonpte.com/

http://www.cambridgeenglish.org/exams/advanced/
https://www.ets.org/toefl/ibt/about
https://www.occupationalenglishtest.org/
https://www.border.gov.au/Trav/Stud/More/Student-Visa-English-Language-Requirements

### 15 Admission Interview

https://www.studyinaustralia.gov.au/

## Section 3

### 16 Overview of Visa Application

https://www.border.gov.au/Trav/Visa/
https://www.border.gov.au/Lega/Lega/Help/how-to-pay

### 19 Medical Checkup

https://www.border.gov.au/Lega/Lega/Help/Location/india
http://www.border.gov.au/Trav/Visa/Heal/meeting-the-health-requirement/health-examinations/my-health-declarations

### 20 Overseas Student Health Cover

http://ahmoshc.com/english.aspx
https://www.nib.com.au/overseas-students
http://oshc.bupa.com.au/
https://www.medibank.com.au/overseas-health-insurance/oshc/
https://allianzassistancehealth.com.au/en/

### 22 GTE Facts, Criteria and Evaluation

www.payscale.com

### 27 Application for your Spouse

https://www.border.gov.au/Trav/Stud/Brin

## Section 4

### 28 Travel

https://www.casa.gov.au/safety-management/landing-page/advice-air-travellers

## 29 Accommodation

http://urbanest.com.au/
http://www.iglu.com.au/
https://www.yha.com.au/
http://www.homestaynetwork.org/agents/programs/

## 30 Food and Cooking

https://www.desimarket.com.au/indian-restaurants
https://www.desimarket.com.au/indian-grocery-stores
http://www.hindustan.com.au/about-us.aspx

## 32 Clothing

http://www.bom.gov.au/
http://www.colgate.com.au/app/PDP/LaundryCare/AU/laundry-washing-tips-and-tricks.cvsp

# Section 5

## 36 Managing Money

www.seek.com.au
www.indeed.com.au
www.gumtree.com.au
https://www.isiccard.com.au/
https://taxfilenumberaustralia.com.au

## Migration Pathways after completing your studies in Australia

### Medium and Long-term Strategic Skills List (MLTSSL)

https://www.border.gov.au/Trav/Work/Work/Skills-assessment-and-assessing-authorities/skilled-occupations-lists/mltssl

### Short-term Skilled Occupation List (STSOL)

http://www.border.gov.au/Trav/Work/Work/Skills-assessment-and-assessing-authorities/skilled-occupations-lists

### Immigration Hotspot Australia

www.immigrationhotspot.com.au

# Appendix 2: List of universities in Australia

## 2 State-wise Universities in Australia

http://www.studyinaustralia.gov.au/global/australian-education/universities-and-higher-education/list-of-australian-universities